A SELF-REGULATION SOCIAL SKILLS WORKBOOK FOR CHILDREN

Over 75 Proven CBT activities and exercises to help children manage big emotions, control anger, develop effective communication skills, and calm anxiety

Age Range: 8-14 years

AMY RYMS

Copyright © 2023 Amy Ryms

All rights reserved. This publication, or any part thereof, may not be reproduced in any form or by any means, including electronic, photographic, or mechanical, or by any sound recording system, or by any device for storage and retrieval of information, without the written permission of the copyright owner.

Disclaimer

We want to make sure you understand the purpose of this document clearly. It is designed to provide you with educational and entertaining information. We have taken great care to ensure that the information presented is accurate, reliable, and up-to-date.

However, it's important to note that this document does not offer any guarantees or warranties. The author is not providing legal, financial, medical, or professional advice. The content has been compiled from various sources to help you gain a better understanding of the subject matter.

We strongly advise you to consult with a licensed professional before attempting any techniques or actions mentioned in this document. Your safety and well-being are our top priority, and professional guidance is crucial.

By reading this document, you agree that the author cannot be held responsible for any direct or indirect losses that may occur as a result of using the information provided. This includes but is not limited to errors, omissions, or inaccuracies. We encourage you to use your own judgment and take personal responsibility for any decisions made based on the information contained within this document.

Contents

Introduction 8

Chapter One: What Are Emotions? 14

    Examples of Emotions 16

    How Do I Feel? 19

    What are Strong Emotions? 22

    Anger as a Strong Emotion 25

    Anxiety as a Strong Emotion 35

    Ever Heard of the Word *Frustration*? 38

Chapter Two: Am I Too Young to Feel Strong Emotions? 43

    You're Not Too Young to Feel Angry 44

    Where Does Anger Come From? 45

    How Your Anger Lets You Know That It's There 47

    Anxiety Happens Even to Younger Children 51

    Why Am I Ashamed of Expressing My Strong Feelings? 55

    Should I Deny My Emotions at Any Time? 57

Embrace Your Emotions Because They're Yours 61

Chapter Three: Questions and Answers About Emotions 64

Do Other Children Also Feel Strong Emotions? 65

Where Do These Emotions Come From? 66

Where Do They Go? 68

Can Strong Emotions Be Controlled? 69

Is Yelling Alright When I'm Angry or Stressed?............. 72

Is it Possible to Always Understand How I'm Feeling?. 75

Chapter Four: Venting Emotions With Communication Skills... 78

Why Effective Communication is Vital Even at a Young Age 79

How to Improve Communication Skills 82

Communication Games and Activities............................ 87

Six Engaging Child Games and Activities 88

Six Communication Games and Exercises for Young Children.. 91

Seven Engaging Student Games and Exercises 93

Five Nonverbal Communication Games and Activities 98

Chapter Five: Calming My Anger.................................. 102

    Where Does It Feel?.. 104

    How I Feel When I'm Angry 105

    What Happens to My Body When I'm Angry? 106

    It's Dangerous to Let Your Anger Run Wild 107

    Exercises for Calming Anger.............................. 114

Chapter Six: Calming My Anxiety 130

    What Are Worries? 130

    Where Do My Worries Come From? 134

    Where Do I Feel My Anxiety?........................... 137

    How Do I Calm My Anxiety 138

Chapter Seven: Calming My Stress................................... 145

    What is Stress?... 147

    What Causes Stress? 147

    What Stresses You Out?..................................... 148

    Stress Relief Activities and Exercises for Children 149

    Components of Children's Art Therapy........................ 160

Chapter Eight: Other People Feel Emotions, Too........... 163

    What is Empathy.. 165

Empathy Check-In 166

It's Not All About Us.. 168

Caring Connects Us to Others.. 171

Empathy in Action 176

Chapter Nine: I'll Be Myself and Nothing Else 194

Practice Positive Self-Talk 195

Morning Meditations 202

Evening Meditations 204

Bedtime Meditation Script.. 206

Helpful Exercises for Staying Calm and in Charge of My Feelings 208

Creative Calm-Down Tips for Children 211

Final Words 223

References 225

Introduction

Everybody in the world is seeking happiness — and there is one sure way to find it. That is by controlling your thoughts. Happiness doesn't depend on outward conditions. It depends on inner conditions.

Dale Carnegie

Children are humans — they develop feelings too. Eleven-year-old Billy was once so angry that he refused to eat. He felt angry because Sophie, his mom, didn't want him to play video games.

Ranting, he said, "You always do this! I hate you!" Knowing he shouldn't have expressed hatred towards mom, he came back thirty minutes later to apologize.

Hugging Sophie, Billy said, "I was wrong, mom. I shouldn't talk like that." Sophie replied, "It's okay, son. I was hoping you would complete your homework before playing games."

If you're reading this, your child is probably going

through a battle with anger, frustration, or another explosive emotion, and the situation may seem hopeless. The issue may even be causing your child to cut ties with friends and relatives. You're aware they need support but don't know where to go.

Maybe you've been searching for a book that will perfectly suit your children but haven't found any that matches their taste. Your friends recommended some because they knew people who used them to achieve robust child-parent relationships. After reading the books, you didn't get the results you wanted.

You are experiencing difficulty in understanding your child and need help knowing how a child feels in different situations. You've searched the internet and consulted your friends for ideas, but nothing seems to be working.

Would finding a book that teaches your child to manage or improve their emotions using self-regulation strategies make you happy? Would you encourage your children to try them if you're given valuable resources for young children to get comfortable with their feelings and behave well when angry or frustrated? Would you feel better if your children were more balanced and adept at coping with anger and sudden outbursts?

With this book, you will learn to help your child manage their emotions simply and realistically. When they are ready, you may assist them in realizing their full potential, fulfilling their greatest dreams, and exploring the realm of successful self-regulation practice.

The detailed guide in this book will give your child step-by-step instructions on how to create and maintain their self-regulation activities. Reading and applying this book's strategies will also:

- Help you learn what causes emotional outbursts in children

- Teach you and your child creative strategies to manage your child's feelings using self-regulation methods

- Provide you with a simplified CBT workbook that perfectly suits your child

- Supplement your learning with a valuable guide including several helpful exercises your child will love and enjoy

- Assist you in understanding your child better and bonding with them more intimately, thus helping them grow into a balanced and happy human

This book is divided into three parts. The first part focuses on helping children get comfortable with strong feelings, emphasizing that they're not too young to feel those emotions.

The second part expressly discusses the Cognitive Behavioral Therapy (CBT) principles incorporated into exercises and workbook questions to help children deal with anger, stress, and anxiety amidst other strong emotions.

The third and last section of the book teaches kids how to better control their emotions by using positive self-talk, meditation techniques, and additional self-confidence-building activities.

Inside this book, you're going to learn everything about emotions: why and how you can feel strong emotions as a young kid, how to vent emotions without sacrificing effective communication, how to feel heard and valued, and how to calm your anger, anxiety, and stress.

You will have access to over 75 CBT-based exercises and games to improve both self-regulation and social skills.

Learning such skills will help you and your child develop the confidence to be yourselves. This book will give you an advantage as a beginner in the world of learning and using cognitive behavioral therapy exercises for your children who need to master their outbursts and frustrations.

After reading this book and encouraging your child to apply it, you will see positive changes in how your child manages their emotions. Help your child start their learning right away, and the next time they come face to face with a frustrating situation, they'll know what to do.

As an authority who loves helping people overcome issues with their children's development, particularly those on the emotional or mental stability of the child, Amy Ryms has mentored many caregivers and children.

Besides being a successful coach who has helped scores of teenagers and young adults overcome physical, mental, and emotional challenges, Amy Ryms knows what they're talking about—they have been studying the best methods for teaching children to manage their emotions and avoid harmful outbursts for over five years.

Helping you achieve freedom from frustration when dealing with your child matters deeply to Amy Ryms. What you're about to learn helped them overcome their own struggles with these issues and be better at showing their children how to be more stable using CBT techniques. Amy Ryms understands how difficult it might seem to help your child handle their emotional issues on your own, and as such, they can show you how to work things out while experiencing minimal stress.

The purpose of this book is to convey the valuable strategies of CBT therapy in an easily digestible way to struggling parents everywhere. Join Amy Ryms as they discuss practical ways parents can collaborate with their children to manage or prevent physical, mental, and emotional outbursts. Your self-regulation and social skill journey starts in Chapter One with "What are Emotions?"

Chapter One:

What Are Emotions?

Have you ever noticed how happy you look on certain days? You're eager to spend time with your pals and engage in all of your favorite activities. Those days were very fantastic times. You've undoubtedly also observed that on some days, you don't feel particularly amused.

Even playing with your pals and eating your favorite meal might not be something you want to do. You would want to skip those days, don't you? You're experiencing something, whether smiling, laughing, or relaxing by yourself.

What distinguishes feelings from emotions, exactly? When something alarming happens, your body reacts with emotions (Day, 2022). When someone yells *Boo*, for example, you might jump and get scared. Such emotion may be followed by a feeling. You can be upset because the *boo* caused you to spill your beverage.

Your moods and emotions can impact your day's events. You experience many brand-new and unique events daily. You experience a wide range of emotions when you encounter these situations. Some emotions are positive, while others are less so.

Having a wide range of emotions and feelings is very natural. And guess what? You are not alone. Everyone you know has lots of emotions.

Your feelings can affect how you behave at home with your family, in school with your teachers and classmates, and when you're hanging out with your friends. Emotions and feelings are such a big part of life that it's important to understand them and where they come from. It's really helpful, too. Once you learn what you're feeling and why you should know how to deal with it, you'll also be able to express or share those feelings with others in a healthy way instead of just bottling them up inside you. I promise you. You'll feel much better once you do!

Examples of Emotions

We display or manage emotions differently; what makes someone furious may not alter another person's behavior or temperament. Still, everyone (regardless of age or gender) expresses certain emotions. Let's talk about six of the biggest emotions that everyone experiences. These emotions can lead you to have lots of different feelings, too.

Happiness. When you feel happy, you might smile or laugh. You might even dance and sing your favorite song. Happiness makes you feel good about things in your life, like school, your friends, and that test you aced this morning.

Surprise. You might feel surprised when something happens that you didn't expect. You might scrunch your forehead or even jump when you feel surprised. A surprise can make you feel happy, but it can also make you nervous.

Fear. When you think you're in danger or feel like

something bad might happen, you experience fear. If you see a big spider, you might feel afraid. Reporting in front of the class can make you feel this way. You may jump back and throw something at a spider or feel goosebumps or a stomach ache.

Sadness. When you feel sad, you might cry or want to be alone. This feeling can happen if you lose a pet or even a toy. You might also feel sad about being called names by someone at school or about not making the soccer team.

Anger. Did you ever feel like exploding or blowing off? If you did, you've probably experienced anger. Anger comes when something happens that you don't like. You might feel angry if somebody is being unfair, if you break a favorite toy, or if your mom says you can't sleep over at your friend's house.

Disgust. When you are disgusted, you might feel like you want to throw up. This emotion can happen when someone does something super gross. It can also happen when you see or smell something that stinks.

More Emotions!

Okay, you're on a roll with the big six emotions—but there are so many more! Look at the emotions below to see other emotions that people always feel.

shy, bored, angy, anxious
happy, tired, surprised, sad
confused, sleepy, crazy, nervous
curious, disappointed, stubbon, hate

See how many emotions and feelings there are? And these are just a few! I bet you can find some on the wheel that you've had before — probably loads of times. If it's your first time meeting someone, you could feel awkward or shy. You might feel confused when a friend stops being nice to you or jealous when your dog chooses to sleep in your little brother's room every night. The ways you can feel are endless. It is perfectly natural to feel all of these feelings. We all feel them.

How Do I Feel?

Think about how you feel right now. Consider how you felt this morning. Do you feel the same way, or do you feel different somehow? Our feelings are constantly changing because new things are always happening. Highlight the feelings that best describe how you've felt today and over the last couple of days.

Happy

Excited

Afraid

Worried

Embarrassed

Confused

Loved

Proud

Nervous

Confident

Silly

Sad

Angry

Shy

Surprised

Think about each word you highlighted. Then use each one to complete this sentence:

I felt ---------------------- when -----------------------------
----

Did you learn anything? Did any of your answers surprise you?

My Emotional Score

How well do you understand emotions? Don't be nervous! This isn't a test. Read the statement, and then decide if that statement describes YOU never, sometimes, or often.

I can tell when a situation is making me upset by how

my body feels.

a) Never

b) Sometimes

c) Often

When I feel angry, I do something to calm myself, like breathing or counting.

a) Never

b) Sometimes

c) Often

I can tell how other people are feeling by looking at their faces and what their bodies are doing.

a) Never

b) Sometimes

c) Often

I help my friends with their hard feelings by giving good advice and being a good example.

a) Never

b) Sometimes

c) Often

For an A, you should award yourself one point, two points for a B, and three points for a C.

What's your score?............

If your score was 4-5, you could really benefit from getting to know your emotions better, and this book will show you how. Keep reading to learn more!

If your score was 6-10, you are close to understanding your emotions. Keep reading to increase your score even more!

If your score was 11-12: You greatly understand your emotions. Keep reading this book to make it even better.

What are Strong Emotions?

We all have strong emotions, so be assured that occasionally feeling overwhelmed by a particularly strong emotion is very normal. When you exhibit irrational behavior due to being incredibly excited, scared, or angry, you are experiencing a strong emotion.

Although they are a vital component of who you are,

emotions may occasionally be messy, difficult, and downright perplexing. A crucial component of achieving emotional wellness is learning to identify and discuss your feelings with others and yourself.

Here are examples of strong emotions:

Anger

Fear

Sadness

Disgust

Happiness

Anger as a Strong Emotion

Barbies. Legos. Stuffed animals. What's your choice of toys? Playing with toys is fun and every kid's delight. But how will you feel if someone (maybe your younger brother or their friend) enters your room and takes away your favorite toy without permission? Would you scream or feel like hitting them?

Suppose a friend borrowed your dearest toy and broke it; you'd probably get angry.

Sometimes, feeling furious is helpful and healthy. It alerts children when something isn't fair or proper and helps children stand up for themselves when treated unfairly. The hard part is knowing how to deal with these strong feelings.

Anger becomes a problem when a child's behavior turns aggressive or gets out of control. A kid's anger may not be open to them or their caregivers. As a parent, assisting in identifying likely sources of rage in children helps (NHS, n.d.).

What Exactly is Anger?

From seeing relatives yell or fight one another to facing academic or test difficulties, children face different emotions. Being harassed or having strong feelings of worry, stress, or terror towards something often makes children furious.

Anger occurs when you display displeasure or annoyance feelings toward someone or objects you believe have wronged you. It has its benefits — it helps release unpleasant emotions or inspires answers to issues (APA, n.d.).

While it is acceptable to be angry, learning to express your anger appropriately is key.

What Aids Anger?

Many children are furious when facing many difficult

assignments or chores. Some get mad quickly when bullied. Suppose you lose an important game or struggle to understand your homework—you may feel upset with yourself since frustration is one of the common causes of anger (Children Health, 2018).

You may be angry if other children make fun of you or laugh at you. If a teacher or parent blames you for something you know nothing about, you may become enraged. Oftentimes children become angry so quickly and intensely that they don't realize why they are angry or they can't put words to it.

As a parent, you can help your children spot and manage their anger by working together. Helping children deal with fury can be amusing and inventive. Your actions when angry may influence how your child responds. You'll both gain from doing it together.

How Can I Know I'm Angry?

Learning to identify the warning signs of anger early can help children make better choices and control their rage. Children express anger differently; for example, while some children breathe faster or stiffen their muscles when furious, others feel as if their stomach is turning.

Your body has a way of alerting you when there is trouble. If your body is tense, you're breathing more quickly, or you want to hit someone or something, you are angry. Anger could make you scream or yell at someone, including people you like or love.

Some people keep their rage buried deep within them. If you do this, you may experience headaches or stomach pain. You might feel bad about yourself or start crying. Find a constructive way to vent your anger without harming anyone or yourself.

How to Identify Angry Friends or People

If you are talking to someone (or asking them questions) and they walk away, become silent and withdrawn, or stop speaking to you, they may be angry. Some people scream and attempt to hit or harm those nearby. If someone is this enraged, you should leave as soon as possible.

If you hurt someone, they might feel bad or get angry. After they're calm or willing to talk, walk up to them and apologize.

Sometimes, helping someone to enhance their mood requires understanding their problem and emotion. Ask yourself, "What do they think?" and "Why do they behave that way?" Knowing what's causing or impacting a friend's troubles is necessary before you can offer support.

Remember this: allow the angry person to calm down before discussing the issue. If they're telling you something, please pay attention to show you care about them.

How Anger Hurts Us

Miguel thought his sister might pick a show he liked. But, nope, she picked something he didn't like—just like always! And not only that, she picked something she KNEW he didn't like. Worst of all, she didn't even pay attention to the show! And then, she got distracted and knocked over their milk and cookies.

Now, Miguel is infuriated. Why does his sister

always have to ruin everything? Because of her, he lost his TV time and didn't have the snack he liked. He decides he will do something to get even with his sister.

He finds a drawing she made earlier that day in her preschool class. He picks it up and rips her drawing into pieces. As he does, he thinks about how unfair everything always is. This will show her! When his sister comes and sees her drawing all torn up, she begins to cry. She tells Miguel she made the drawing for him as a surprise.

Miguel now feels guilty, embarrassed, and ashamed. He thinks to himself, "I guess I didn't have to ruin her art because I was mad." His anger then turns to himself. "What's wrong with me," he thinks. He begins to cry. His father comes into the room and yells that he is very disappointed with Miguel. As punishment, Miguel loses his TV time for the rest of the week.

In this story, Miguel lets his anger meter get too high. He let his anger out by ruining an object and hurting his sister's feelings. There are many things Miguel could have done instead. For example, he could have shared how he was feeling.

The Helpful Side of Anger

Anger DOES have a good side. Here are a few things anger helps us with:

- Anger protects us and the people we care about from danger.
- Anger lets us know that something is not right.
- Anger helps us realize we feel something is unfair.
- Anger lets us know we are not okay with how someone is treating us.
- Anger lets other people know that we are upset.

Can you share two times when anger has helped you?

Sometimes, we think that if anger gets us what we want, it's helpful. Imagine a little girl in a store screaming for candy, and her mother buys it for her. It might seem like screaming helped the girl get what she wanted. Right then, it did help her get the candy. But this taught her that she could scream and get angry to get what she wanted. That is not a good lesson, and it's not helpful.

Let's go back to the story about Miguel getting angry at his sister. Where in the story did he have a chance to do something else with his anger? For example, could he have shared his feelings, redirected his thoughts, or done something else to let his anger out?

Here are some ideas of things Miguel could have done:

- He could have shared with his parents that he felt it was unfair and was having difficulty releasing his anger.
- He could have remembered that it would be his turn to pick a show the next time.
- He could have thought that what his sister liked was just as important as what he liked.
- He could have used one of the body exercises to get his anger out.
- He could have done target practice.
- He could have done the towel twist.
- He could have looked at his secret anger list to get ideas.
- He could have thought about how he would feel if his sister got angry at him just for picking his favorite

show to watch.

Do you have any other ideas of things Miguel could have done when he got angry?

The Tricky Side of Anger

Anger often makes us feel very powerful. Have you ever felt that way? Sometimes, we say mean things that hurt other people's feelings. Sometimes, we even say mean things about ourselves. We also might hurt other people or ourselves or break things. The more anger builds up in our bodies, the more likely it is to come out in hurtful ways.

When this happens, we might feel super powerful and like we have control. But the way to wrangle our anger is to use helpful ways to get it out instead of hurtful ones.

Let's do an activity to see how anger can build up and make us feel tired and weak. First, stand up and straighten your arms like a zombie or Frankenstein's monster.

The grown-up reading this book will start putting pillows in your arms that you need to hold up (blankets or other objects that are easy to stack can also be used.) They will start with one pillow, wait a few seconds, add another, and keep going.

Each time a pillow is placed on your arms, think of something that makes you angry. Then say the thing out loud. But make sure you don't shout in the grown-up's ear! Try to get to at least five pillows—because anger is huge! Hold the pile as long as you can. When you feel they are about to fall, throw them down.

Your arms probably got wiggly or achy after holding the pillows. Do you feel strong and powerful right now or tired and exhausted? Tired, right? This is often how we feel after anger takes over.

We won't be so exhausted if we practice letting anger out in helpful ways. That will give us more time to do fun things!

This activity is a good one to do when you are already angry. You can say out loud all the things that are making you angry. When you throw down the pillows, imagine you are throwing away the anger.

Anxiety as a Strong Emotion

Anyone can feel anxious, so don't assume it only affects children and teenagers. Your body reacts to stress by producing anxiety: a feeling of fear or dread of what lies ahead. You may experience anxiety when delivering a speech, moving to a new place, or taking an exam (Holland, 2022).

Your brain releases adrenaline, the anxiety hormone, after sensing possible threats or attacks. Anxiety is common and important for survival when exposed to risky or troubling situations. But get support if your stress symptoms are getting serious or persistent (Felman, 2020).

Each person experiences anxiety differently, but possible feelings to expect when stressed include stomach pains and a speeding heart. Worry is an emotion; it could be small or large. Everyone develops both minor and major concerns from time to time.

Many different words are used to describe the sensation of anxiety. Here are a few examples:

Stress

panic

Jumpiness

Insecurity

phobia

Butterflies

Inner turmoil

Fright

Nervousness

Tension

Grab a notebook and a pen and survey the individuals closest to you to help understand anxiety. It might be your mother, father, or grandparents. Then, write down their responses on separate pieces of paper after you ask them the following questions.

What word from the list best depicts anxiety? (Read or show them the list above.)

……………………………………..

Do you consider yourself highly, moderately, or rarely anxious, and why?

…………………………………..

Describe how you experience anxiety in your body, mind, and emotions.

…………………………………..

Now, pose the same questions to yourself and record your responses here:

…………………………………..

…………………………………..

What have you learned so far?

…………………………………..

Ever Heard of the Word *Frustration*?

Many young children find it difficult to tolerate frustration. Children's reactions can be fierce in the heat of the moment since anger and frustration are strong emotions. Adults are aware of when their anger buttons are being pressed. We know the steps we must take to resolve a frustrating situation effectively. However, children do not come into this world with a bag full of techniques for controlling their anger.

It takes time and repetition to develop coping mechanisms for dealing with frustration.

The good news is that parents may assist children in developing patience for irritation at home. You can train your child to handle difficult situations with a little direction (and a lot of patience).

Do some body mapping. Children in their early years do not connect their physical and emotional states. For instance, I am aware that a painful neck indicates tension. Knowing this, I can take a minute to consider what I should do to reduce my stress. Children find it difficult to reach those conclusions. They might clench their fists and get aching muscles, but they won't pause to consider how their emotional moods may be causing those sore muscles.

One of the best techniques from The Happy Child Handbook is body mapping, which benefits children of all ages (MHC., 2014). Draw a person's outline (or, if you're like me, search online and print). Ask your child to list every part of his body that hurts or feels different when angry. You can mention how becoming angry makes your heart race and makes you feel lightheaded. It's crucial to do this activity with your child. Color your heart and head red. Tell your child that if those areas start to red, his body is telling him to seek assistance in a trying situation.

Learn what sparks the frustration. Although every child is unique and may experience frustration in different ways, there are a few typical ones to look out for

- Transitions
- Bad peer relationships (or perceived negative interactions)
- Academic challenges (even for young children — using scissors may be quite difficult)
- A sense of being misunderstood by peers or adults
- No self-control
- Hunger or exhaustion

- Unexpected circumstances

By maintaining a tracker, you may assist your child in understanding their particular issues. Note what happened before the incident, the time of day, and what was going on when the meltdown occurred.

Make a crazy list. A crazy list was the key to letting my child let out his rage when he was younger. Young children require venting (just like adults), but they lack the skills to do so. In the heat of the moment, screaming and writhing feel fantastic, so they stick with it.

Demand that your child lists all of the things that irritate him. While expressing his feelings, he should write his list on paper. While doing this, show compassion and comprehension. A simple "Ooh, that makes me furious, too!" might help children feel understood and that they are being heard. Ask your child to cut the list into tiny pieces when it is finished so they can throw them in the air as a much-needed physical release of emotion. After that, gather the fragments and dispose of them.

Teach the stoplight while breathing deeply. The importance of deep breathing has undoubtedly been brought up frequently and for a good reason. Deep breathing may effectively soothe a child's senses and enable the child to process a distressing situation without shouting.

Deep breathing exercises are best performed when both of you are at ease. Unfortunately, children often mistake deep breathing for quick breathing until they get the hang of it, which has the opposite impact.

Request that your child sit quietly and loosen his muscles. When your child inhales, count to four. When he holds his breath, count to three. When he exhales, count to four. Repeat a few times, then do this often (bonus tip: this also works wonders for worriers). I like to have my children "breathe the rainbow" by having them focus on one color while taking a deep breath (strawberries, cherries, and bouncy balls, oh my!).

Teach the stoplight next. Red denotes a stop, yellow denotes a slowdown, and green denotes a forward motion. Take it a step further by instructing them on how to stop at a red light when they are feeling frustrated. They might use deep breathing to unwind their bodies and thoughts during this time. Make a large stoplight out of construction paper and attach it to your refrigerator as a guide. The meltdowns will eventually stop when this procedure becomes automatic.

Dealing with negative feelings could be a challenging task for children; however, it's important for children to communicate their problems to trusted adults. Problems can be prevented or made to feel less troubling for the child if they open up to their parents or caregivers when battling with strong emotions. This sometimes requires child-parent collaboration—as a parent, teach your child to spot and label their emotions. If they have anything to share with you, be eager to hear them out without judgment.

Remember that you are your kid's first role model. They are studying your steps and learning from you at this critical stage of their life. Show your child how to manage their feelings through your lifestyle. Your child will know whether they're too young to feel strong emotions in the next chapter.

Chapter Two:

Am I Too Young to Feel Strong Emotions?

If you have seen two or three-year-olds display strong emotions, you are not alone. When my brother's boy was this old, his demand for attention was so high that his mom had to stop working. This chapter is crucial to letting young children know they're not too young to feel strongly about a situation. It discusses that anger, anxiety, stress, frustration, and other emotions are as valid as happiness, joy, confidence, gratitude, and the like.

You're Not Too Young to Feel Angry

Bailey is at a bakery with her aunt. They wait in line for her favorite breakfast food—a cinnamon bun. Yum! Someone cuts in line in front of them. When Bailey and her aunt get to the counter, they are told that the bakery just sold the last cinnamon roll. There are only cranberry oat muffins left. Yuck!

"This is so unfair," Bailey thinks to herself. She stares at the person who cut in line, eyeing the cinnamon bun they have in their hand. She feels even worse as she watches the cinnamon bun thief smile and takes a big bite. Isn't it enough that they took what should have been hers? Now, they have to rub it in?

Bailey kicks the trash can next to her. Her aunt looks at her, frowns, and says, "Why do you have to get angry all the time? This is a treat. If you can't be nice, we will be leaving."

"Oh, great. Now, I'm in trouble!" Anger takes over Bailey's body. She kicks the trash can again. She feels like she can't stop herself. At that point, her aunt has had enough and takes her home.

Bailey didn't get her cinnamon bun—or any treat at

all. And she was sure a lecture from her parents would be coming next. Have you ever experienced something similar? In life, many things happen that feel unfair. These things can then make us feel many different feelings, including anger. But if we can change how we think about something that happens to us, it will change how we feel!

Bailey was doing what we call extreme thinking. Extreme thinking happens when we think there are only two choices: "It's fair" or "It's unfair." But if we think about a situation differently or add more choices or thoughts, it can change how we feel.

For example, after her outburst, Bailey could have thought, "It's okay. People make mistakes, and I made a mistake." She could have told her aunt how she was feeling and asked if they could go to another bakery for a cinnamon roll.

Where Does Anger Come From?

Everyone gets angry sometimes, and that's okay. But what is anger? Anger is one of the many feelings or emotions we feel in our brains and bodies. Anger helps protect us. But when we are young and learning to control it, anger can be very tricky. When we first learn to work on our anger, it can feel like the anger monster goes from sleeping to doing flips on a trampoline in less than two seconds!

Has your anger ever gotten really big, really fast, so you felt like you had no control? Sometimes, the anger can feel like it comes from nowhere, but something usually happens first for it to come.

The list below describes ordinary things that might wake up the anger monster. For this activity, start by standing. For each thing that has woken your anger monster, clap your hands or jump up and down.

- Someone took your toy.
- A grown-up told you no.
- A friend or brother or sister was mean to you.
- You didn't get to do something you wanted to do.
- You didn't get something you thought you would get.
- You felt left out.
- No one listened to you.
- Something wasn't fair.

- You felt like other people didn't understand you.

Good job! What did you learn? Did you discover anything that surprised you?

How Your Anger Lets You Know That It's There

Anger lets us know it's there and needs our attention in many ways. One way that we know that the anger monster is gaining more control is when we start thinking a lot of icky or negative thoughts. Or we start having extreme thoughts. For example, we might think, Why even try? There's no point. Or I will never be able to control my anger.

Nicholas is at recess. His best friend, Ali, promises to play tag, but Nicholas sees her playing jump rope. Nicholas continues to play, but he wonders why Ali is not playing with him.

Nicholas feels his cheeks becoming warm, and he is suddenly hot all over his body. He begins to remember all the times Ali made him angry. His tummy feels like Nicholas ate a brick. He tightens his hands into fists, and his arms shake. He wants to punch something but knows he will get in trouble.

Nicholas sees a basketball near him. Without thinking, he kicks it in Ali's direction. He wants to get her attention, but the ball hits Ali in the knee instead of zipping past her. She falls to the ground.

Nicholas runs off and hides behind a tree. Ali is crying now, and a teacher helps her get up. Nicholas feels his cheeks are wet, burying his face in the grass. He didn't mean to hurt anyone. But sometimes, he feels like he has no control over his anger. His parents often tell him he has "anger problems." They ask him, "Why can't you just control it?" But how do you control something that feels out of control?

In this story, Nicholas felt different reactions in his body. Nicholas felt hot in his cheeks, and tears came out of his eyes. His tummy did not feel good. His hands became tight fists, and his arms were shaking.

The list below describes different reactions children have when anger comes. For this activity, start by standing up. Each time you hear a reaction that has happened to you, act it out or point to where you feel it in your body. For example, you could squeeze your hands very tight or point to your tummy.

You might feel:

- Hotness in your face or another part of your body
- Tightness in your hands, arms, legs, face, or another part of your body
- An icky feeling in your tummy
- Like your hands, feet, or legs need to hit or kick
- Heart beating very fast
- Sweating
- Crying
- Shaking in your hands, arms, legs, or another part of your body
- A weight in your heart or stomach
- Wanting to throw up
- Needing to use the restroom
- A headache

Great job! It's important to know how your body feels when anger comes. Your body might even know when you are angry before you do! So, if you notice your body acting angrily, you can try to do something before the anger monster takes over.

Secret Anger List

When we are angry, it can be very hard to think about the things that will help us calm down. When someone is angry, they sometimes say it feels like their brain is not working properly. You know what? That is sort of true!

When we are super angry, the thinking part of our brain does not work very well. This means that when we are really angry, it's hard to think of something to do to help the anger.

For this activity, list all the actions you might be willing to try when you are angry.

To get you started, here is a list of different actions. Activities from this chapter are included. If you have other ideas, go ahead and add them.

Run around your backyard five times.

Do jumping jacks.

Throw a ball at a target.

Use playdough, clay, a fidget toy, or a stress ball.

Go into your room, and hit a pillow.

Stomp up and down.

Jump on a trampoline. Listen to your favorite music.

Rip up a paper.

………………………………..

………………………………..

………………………………..

Now grab a piece of paper. Make your own secret list that you can look at. Or, if you want, a grown-up can show you the list when the anger monster takes control. You can then pick something to do with your anger that will be helpful.

Anxiety Happens Even to Younger Children

Anxiety is when you feel worried or nervous. Your stomach might hurt. You might shake a little or have a hard time talking. This might happen because your brain gets confused. It thinks you're in danger even if you are not (NHS Inform, 2019).

Allan can't stop worrying about a project for school. He has to speak in front of his class. He doesn't like the sound of it. He feels terrible in his belly whenever he remembers the project and feels sick and scared. He wonders if he can pretend to be sick to get out of the project.

His big sister, Tibby, notices Allan acting funny. She asks him what is wrong, and after a little while, Allan tells her. Tibby understands why Allan is scared and nervous. She remembered doing the project herself last year. She tells Allan this.

"Allan, I was scared when I had to talk in front of my

class, too. A lot of children are. But that's okay. Doing the things that scare you can be a good learning experience."

"Yeah, but I am still nervous!" Allan said.

Tibby nods. "The best thing to do is practice, practice, practice. And remember that everyone else is nervous, too. You're not alone, and the people you have to talk in front of are your friends; they understand how hard it is, too."

Allan thinks about that.

"You are right.

I'm still nervous, but I feel I can do it now because I will not be the only one."

What was Allan worried about for school?

....

Where does Allan feel the terrible feeling in his body?

....

Tibby said the best thing to do is

....

Quick Assessment

Have you recently felt

Worried?

Scared?

Unsure of what to do?

So queasy you might throw up?

Sweaty and clammy?

Frightened about what might happen next?

Jumpy and unsettled?

Like you want to run away?

If you feel any of those things, it's okay. We're all allowed to feel scared sometimes. Everyone gets scared and nervous, even if they are good at hiding it.

One thing to remember is that everyone gets worried. Being worried means you care and think through all the things that might happen. This can keep you safe sometimes because it can remind you to think about what you are doing.

But the tough part comes when the worry and anxiety start taking over your day. Most of the time, being in an anxious state is tiring, mentally and physically. You must live a balanced life, be cautious at times and enjoy life, too!

Why Am I Ashamed of Expressing My Strong Feelings?

I'm Ashamed

Not everyone finds it easy to express their emotions.

Sometimes, obstacles prevent you from expressing yourself, such as:

You have no idea what you're feeling.

You are concerned that it will lead to conflict.

You believe it will have no effect.

You don't want others to be concerned about you.

You're afraid to admit how you feel.

You are concerned that others will judge you negatively.

You believe you should not be feeling this way.

You believe it will be perceived as weak or incapable.

You believe that others should already understand how you feel.

You are concerned about how others will react if you open up.

You don't have anyone you can confide in to express your feelings.

How to Express Yourself

It can start with just two words... **I feel.**

When you're used to keeping your feelings to yourself, it can be difficult to express them.

Remember, saying how you feel is something you can learn to do with practice.

As a starting point, consider the following advice:

Begin with an "I" message, followed by your

emotional word.

I feel…

I felt…

I've been experiencing…

Then describe the situation, event, or action that caused you to feel this way.

When _____, I feel…

I have _____ feelings about…

Want to go one step further? Include why you felt that way or the impact it had on you:

Because _____, I feel _____ when…

Put it all together, and you've expressed your feelings positively and constructively.

For example, I feel upset when I am yelled at because it makes me feel unloved.

Should I Deny My Emotions at Any Time?

We all dislike negative emotions, such as rage, panic, anxiety, depression, disappointment, jealousy, and hatred.

So you try to avoid such emotions, but they come around to you again, no matter where you hide.

What do you do now? If you're like many children, you suppress these feelings. After all, you've been taught that since birth.

Stop crying. Stop talking. Don't say anything. Go to your room.

So instead of crying, you choose to keep your mouth shut, sit in a corner, and spend the entire time in the prison you created for yourself.

It's not that they were incorrect in telling you all of this. Even though it hurts you, you learn to suppress your emotions.

It turns out that suppressing your emotions is not the best way to manage them. It could be harmful to you.

Why Do Children Hide Their Feelings?

If you observe a very young trauma-free child, you'll see that they are honest—they have natural emotional thoughts and responses. They naturally feel excited, inspired, and creative when they are happy, and their needs are satisfied. When children are hurt (or sense danger), they cry or run for safety. They usually don't conceal their emotions. Adults often disregard this natural order—they frown at it or punish children for it.

Children believe lying is the best course of action for adjusting to and surviving in environments where emotions attract punishments. This is common when children live in societies where deceit is accepted.

Children lie and hide their feelings because of these reasons:

Penalty for being honest. Children are instructed not to speak when they observe something that could embarrass their parents or caregivers. They receive direct punishment or rejection if they disregard the instruction. Many parents compromise a child's sincerity in favor of their comfort.

Being doubted or made fun of. Adults don't attach much importance to what children say or think. Sometimes when a child says they've been abused, the people in their lives don't give their concerns proper attention, which often results in exposing the child to further harm. Doubting children (or laughing at them) may prevent them from trusting their parents or caregivers (Cikanavicius, 2018).

Contrasting norms. While some households forbid children from speaking up, they are subjected to inconsistent standards in others. There are cases where children cannot tell the truth. For example, while young people must be truthful about their plans and other private matters, they are expected to keep their opinions to themselves if they witness their father resuming his poor drinking habit, their mother sobbing uncontrollably, or their parents arguing.

Trouble having or expressing particular feelings. Parents may prevent their children from displaying certain emotions. For example, some caregivers punish children for getting angry or sad. Some mock or flog children that mistakenly get injured. So, instead of expressing their feelings, they acquire self-erasing skills (Cikanavicius, 2018).

Poor role models. Children may embrace lying because of the terrible experiences their caregivers set for them. Many adults enjoy lying to children—they play practical jokes, mislead children, invent excuses, and lie when discussing difficult topics.

Children observe people deceive others to achieve their goals and then repeat the pattern themselves by developing those same skills.

Embrace Your Emotions Because They're Yours

As a little kid, my mother always asked, "Why are you crying? There is no need to cry." I grew accustomed to this reaction as I grew older, and it has become how I deal with my reactions to my emotions these days.

I broke down in tears a few months back while chatting with my father about missing a nice pal I hadn't seen because of the epidemic. He noticed me crying and asked, "What's up with the crying?" I cried, not understanding why I was doing it. The truth was that I knew why I was crying, and it was for a good reason. "I don't know either," my father replied, and the conversation ended abruptly. We stopped talking about it instead of my receiving the emotional support I required. However, I am a firm believer in expressing our emotions openly.

Here are reasons why I believe it is important to embrace our emotions:

Showing your emotions fosters trusting relationships. We establish a strong connection and trust when we show others our feelings and give them a glimpse into our emotions. Showing your emotions allows you to connect with the person you're speaking with. You also experience gratitude for being able to get assistance and support.

Changing how you express emotions to one person affects how you interact with others. If you can't express yourself to certain people (in my case, my parents), you might find it difficult to express yourself to others.

Finding common ground. Showing people our true emotions allows us to connect with people we have nothing in common. My friends, who have gone through similar circumstances, have confirmed this. This has allowed us to communicate that we are not alone in our struggles. We can find comfort and support from one another in this way.

So, let it all out. Find something in common with someone. Seek and be a support system for others. Be an example of someone who can express their emotions while remaining a source of strength. Don't let old habits or the reactions of people who may not know how to express themselves harm you. One thing is certain: we are an ever-changing, ever-growing human race, and we must roll with the punches to succeed.

Children can display strong emotions; accepting this helps you to spot and manage your child's emotional outbursts. You will find answers to common emotion questions in the next chapter.

Chapter Three:

Questions and Answers About Emotions

Parents often feel worried if their child exhibits strong emotions earlier than anticipated. They may think, *"What is wrong with my child?"* or *"Why is this child different from other children?"*

Parents may also feel worried if their child continues to exhibit strong emotions when they get older. Sometimes a child's peers will complain about their moods and emotions, making them feel worse and causing the child to wonder if there is something wrong with them. This chapter answers some of the children's most burning questions about emotions.

Do Other Children Also Feel Strong Emotions?

Children have the same emotions as adults. They become angry, frustrated, sad, scared, excited, jealous, and worried, among other emotions. Unfortunately, most children lack the vocabulary to express their emotions clearly.

The other day, we were seated at the kitchen table when I overheard my oldest screaming at his three-year-old sister, "STOP!" Time seemed to stand still. I didn't see anything she did or the buildup. What could have gotten into this child to cause him to dump on his sister?

"Wait a minute, buddy," I wanted to say. "Don't talk to your sister in that manner." Instead, I could see the annoyance on his face, and that he was struggling to identify with the emotions he was experiencing, so I clenched my teeth, breathed deeply, and gently said, "That was loud. It appears that you are upset with your sister. Do you agree with this feeling?"

He said, "No," looking up at me with tears. "I'm not upset. I have no idea what's wrong." Then, I understood that my son didn't have the words to express how he was feeling.

What's the moral of this story? Other children have strong emotions too.

Where Do These Emotions Come From?

Emotions are stored in the limbic system, a region of the brain.

Consider the last time you opened the best gift you've ever received. You may have felt your stomach flip, your heart rate increase, and your face likely turned to a smile. What you felt was happiness, which is also known as feeling an emotion.

Emotions inform us about what we are experiencing. If your childhood pet dies, you may experience sadness. You may feel disgusted if you smell something unpleasant in the garbage can. Basic emotions include anger, fear, joy, and surprise.

Many living things—not just humans—can experience basic emotions. Have you ever seen a dog's tail wagging? Tail wagging is how a dog expresses happiness. However, some emotions are considered higher emotions, such as shame, guilt, and pride, which are only felt by humans and a few other animal species.

Your body and mind will change as a result of any emotion. Emotions are completely natural and change due to various events in our lives.

Where Do They Go?

One of these two ways can be used to explain where emotions go.

First, they move in a way set by cycles that have existed since birth. We can see that an angry outburst often leads to a state of tiredness or, on the other hand, a feeling of separation from the aggressor, which brings peace on its own. When we watch animals, we see signs of emotional cycles similar to ours. When animals fight, they get tired, give in, or split up for a while, but the cycle starts up again when biology lets them.

Second, if you are aware, you can see your feelings and let them go without being so quick to act on them. An experienced meditator may see their anger as it moves through their body and mind. If they stay aware (or mindful), they may be able to see it temporarily disappear over the horizon of their mind. The meditator has calmly watched the cycle, kept it in check, and let it run its course without having to fight anyone else.

Can Strong Emotions Be Controlled?

Yes. Strong emotions can be controlled.

My son was quietly playing in the museum's children's room. He came now and then to show me how tall his tower of wooden blocks was. He was delighted with his colorful creation!

Another child entered the room and ran to the table where he was playing. Then, suddenly, he destroyed my son's tower!

What followed was a tidal wave of rage!

My son wanted to strike the other child, throwing wooden blocks at him. He even attempted to move the entire table to the opposite side of the room.

I was able to stop his attempts, but it wasn't easy to persuade him to sit down with me for a while to calm down.

I saw his red cheeks and clenched fists and knew he was furious.

It wasn't the first time he'd felt such strong emotions. And it was far from the last time!

But, over time, he learned to manage his emotions much better. At the same time, I learned how to better assist him in dealing with strong emotions.

It was extremely difficult for me to assist him during his first tantrums. I was so depressed!

But, thankfully, things improved. We both learned two very important lessons:

First: emotions are neither good nor bad. All emotions are normal, and we should allow ourselves to experience them.

Second: what matters most is how we handle emotions. While we cannot control our feelings, we can control how we behave.

Young children must learn how to manage and control their emotions. Most importantly, they must learn how to make the right decision when overwhelmed by strong emotions.

Every time an emotion overwhelms you, just like my son, sit down and ponder these questions:

What transpired? What made you so angry/upset/sad?

....

How did you feel as a result of this situation?

....

Where did you feel the sadness in your body?

....

How did you react to this feeling?

....

Do you think there's a better way to react when feeling like this?

....

What would be a better option the next time you're in a similar situation?

....

Do you need a big hug to help you get rid of this anger/sadness?

…………………………………………………..

You can always ask your parents or teacher for assistance in answering the questions.

In the end, you will be happy again and willing to act better the next time.

Is Yelling Alright When I'm Angry or Stressed?

Everyone has yelled or shouted in anger at some point in their life. Although some people engage in it frequently, we are all guilty of it occasionally.

Most people utilize yelling as a coping method when they are furious. They express their rage in this way (Biswas, 2020).

We must develop self-control over our anger and yelling to live a long and happy life.

Why Do Children Scream?

Is your child constantly yelling at you when they are upset?

Children's crying may become a habit, which can make parents lose their cool.

If your kid's frequent shouting is causing tension in your home, don't be scared—this is an issue you can fix when you understand the causes. Here are some of the common causes:

Age. Children have a lot of energy—they play different games, explore, and scream when playing with their toys or friends. Shouting or screaming is a natural communication pattern for some children when playing around other children. Since they learn new things daily, shouting helps show their happiness.

Emulating caregivers or family members. Children who yell may be doing so out of imitation of their parent's communication style. So, if you speak loudly, your children may imitate you.

Language issues. Children with speech problems may use yelling to express their feelings.

Getting noticed. A child may use yelling to attract someone's attention. For example, if they feel someone is taking their place, a child might shout to draw attention.

Express feelings. The uneasy emotions your child is experiencing—such as annoyance, jealousy, stress, and even excitement—could be the cause of their screaming.

Children struggle to control the forces that drive these feelings. So, yelling becomes the means of letting them loose.

Developmental phase. Two or three-year-olds often experience temper outbursts—they question parental authority throughout this stage (You are mom, 2019).

Hearing troubles. Children with eardrum inflammation or any hearing problem hardly hear themselves when speaking. This makes them shout.

Finding a solution to your child's constant yelling is possible when the cause is known. Practicing patience helps calm children.

Is it Possible to Always Understand How I'm Feeling?

It could seem nearly unimaginable that someone might be experiencing something they don't understand. But as most people are aware, the phenomenon occurs rather frequently.

The only reliable generalization about all emotions is that they begin life as physiological sensations rather than actual feelings. Therefore, even when people cannot understand their emotional experiences, they are usually conscious of their bodily state. This holds even if all they are experiencing is a "blank" or an odd numbness.

Let's examine more closely why some feelings may be challenging or even impossible to distinguish:

- The emotion hasn't fully developed. When this happens, you're just starting to feel something, but it hasn't yet been clear what it is. It isn't yet recognizable. You might have a physical sensation in your body, such as a constriction in your throat, trembling in your limbs, or an accelerated heartbeat. However, you haven't yet made the connection between bodily activation and the cause of it.

- You're having multiple, strangely "fused" feelings rather than just one. You may feel confused because you are experiencing multiple emotions simultaneously and cannot discriminate between them.

- You've never had this feeling. Because children have not yet reached the stage of development when they can translate their physical experiences into understandable feeling names, children frequently cannot identify what they are feeling.

- The emotion has been suppressed internally: Even when you attempt to access it, nothing comes to mind. It's not difficult to understand why many of us "blacklist" particular emotions. Suppose you were raised in a house where expressing anger was frowned upon and losing your cool could result in severe punishment; you would have learned — almost at a cellular level — that any outward signs of hostility could endanger your vital parental link.

You might have been pressured to suppress all painful emotions if your family made it plain that you weren't to be sad (and not to cry). Fear and worry can also be suppressed if your caregivers tell you these emotions are inappropriate because they indicate weakness or inadequacy.

Knowledge saves life. Knowing the source of a problem is the key to finding the solution. If your child displays strong emotions, encourage them to find out why they're acting that way. If it's something they are struggling to do, give them support. You will learn to manage emotions using your communication skills in the next chapter.

Chapter Four:
Venting Emotions With Communication Skills

The practice of exchanging information between two or more persons in a way that produces the intended outcome is known as effective communication (Help Guide, n.d.). The shared information is sent and received in a clear way that doesn't change its original purpose. It involves skills like nonverbal communication, careful listening, the capacity to understand and regulate one's own emotions, and stress management. This chapter will show you how to have effective and nonviolent communication when big emotions arise and ways to make people hear and validate you and your feelings. It also includes communication games and activities.

Why Effective Communication is Vital Even at a Young Age

Effective communication is a crucial skill; the higher our level of communication, the better our quality of life will be.

We start talking the instant we are born, alerting our mothers with our first cry that we have arrived. It's crucial to foster a child's communication abilities as they grow, so they may express themselves confidently and effectively in all spheres of their lives.

When a child is developing, they first speak with their parents, then their siblings and friends, and then other adults, like their instructors.

Your child will learn to communicate more quickly as you talk to them. Children learn to communicate by observing and imitating their parents' words and actions.

Reading is an excellent practice to help enhance your child's language skills since it exposes them to various words and helps them learn how to speak clearly and easily. As children get older, reading aloud offers a great opportunity for debate, fostering a setting where a child can develop the skills of clearly expressing and exchanging their opinions.

A youngster will acquire social and interpersonal abilities and communication skills through interaction and play with siblings and friends. These abilities will help them feel more at ease in social situations, making it simpler for them to talk to peers and create new acquaintances. Through these partnerships, they will improve their listening abilities, empathy, and capacity for deciphering non-verbal clues.

When a child starts school, they will regularly participate in activities that directly use their verbal communication skills, such as presentations, class discussions, dramatizations, and oral exams. You want a child to feel comfortable in these situations—not just speaking in front of a group of people or making a new friend, but also in their abilities to communicate clearly and leave a positive impression.

A child skilled at verbal communication will find it simpler to write and, as a result, will probably perform better on written projects and tests in school.

Connecting with employers is crucial for anyone looking to the future, regardless of your industry or profession. Nearly every job description lists good communication skills as one of the most coveted traits, and having these talents will put you ahead of your competitors when you apply for new duties.

To land those bigger possibilities effectively, you'll need the communication skills to give orders, run meetings, conduct presentations, and coordinate with customers, clients, and suppliers.

Like any talent, communication skills can be improved with practice. So, by encouraging children to develop strong communication skills early on, you give them the tools they need to build a successful future.

How to Improve Communication Skills

Children in elementary school still learn how to communicate with their peers and develop friends. At this age, your child could require your assistance communicating and learning better ways to express their feelings. Here are ways you can assist your child in improving their communication skills.

Communicate with your child frequently. Children that struggle with communication may not want to speak at all. It will help if you encourage your child to start or join conversations as much as possible. This encouragement will undoubtedly inspire your child to start opening up more.

Discuss your destination with each other in the automobile. Discuss the measures you're doing as you prepare your meals. During the commercial breaks, discuss all of your current favorite TV moments.

Help your child learn how to relate conversational subjects to current events. Always introduce fresh vocabulary and ideas. It could be an example of sentences that your child can use to start conversations.

Describe your day. Encourage your child to describe their day to you in as much detail as possible. What aspects of school were the best and worst? This detail improves recollection and sequencing, two abilities children with difficulty communicating may have trouble with. Also, recount what happened during your day. Say something like, "I went to the grocery store today. Guess what I noticed in the produce section?"

Additionally, sharing in this way fosters a bond between you and your child.

Take note of what your children say and think about it. Demonstrate one of the most crucial conversational skills by focusing on what others say and building on it. After your child has shared something with you, paraphrase a portion of what they said before asking a question. For example: "Wow, that art project sounds like it required a lot of patience. What other project would you find enjoyable to work on? What more supplies would you require?"

Have practice conversations with your child. Discuss the circumstances that your child might be most apprehensive about. These might involve engaging in conversation with other children while awaiting the bus or sitting next to them at lunch, for instance. Then, have your child rehearse possible phrases to consider various scenarios, conversation subjects, and reactions, and take turns pretending to be each other during the conversation.

Highlight nonverbal cues. Children with communication issues might not always be able to read nonverbal clues from other children. These hints are often referred to as *body language.*

Think about demonstrating and explaining body language to your elementary-aged child. The phrases "I'm crossing my arms because I'm upset" or "When you roll your eyes at me, I feel disrespectful" are acceptable.

Engage your child in entertaining talks. Finding engaging subjects to talk about following a busy day might be difficult. Explore the Family Dinner Project's discussion starter suggestions. Additionally, look at some conversational advice for parents:

- "What was the funniest thing you witnessed today at school?"

- "I believe the car needs to be thoroughly cleaned."

- "Should we do it ourselves or take it to a car wash?"

- "What do you want control over? Bumpers? Vacuuming?"

Read out loud to your child. What you read to your child is irrelevant. The most crucial aspect is that you work together. Do not be alarmed if your child consistently selects the same books to read at bedtime. Your youngster is becoming more knowledgeable about the characters, stories, and words.

Read aloud to one another in turns, even if your toddler only adds a few words here and there. Discuss the setting, plot, characters, and unfamiliar words you learned after finishing a book or television program.

Show your child how to play "catch" in a conversation. Try introducing discussions' back-and-forth flow to your child: Here's an illustration:

Player 1 asks a question while hurling a ball. "How is school going?"

Player 2 picks up the ball and responds to the query. Player 2 must then pose another pertinent query before returning the ball. ("Good! How is the math club doing?")

The objective is for your child to become at ease when speaking.

Get your child's perspective. To communicate, children must consider their emotions. Consult your child about daily choices. Simple topics like where to go to the library or how to spend your vacation could be discussed.

Consult your child's viewpoint on pertinent issues. "Should the other team have won?" is one example. "Do you recall recent news stories?" is another. It's also a good idea to practice using "I think" or "I feel" statements to start conversations.

Encourage your child to keep a journal. Once they've had time to process their thoughts, some children find it simpler to communicate with others. Writing about daily activities and emotions in a journal or diary could be beneficial. Due to the process, your child may find it simpler to formulate and communicate ideas. Your child may finally feel more prepared and secure when asked what has been happening.

Communication Games and Activities

Some games, exercises, and activities can help children communicate more effectively. Adults often set social standards and communication styles in most situations. Adults decide on etiquette guidelines as well.

Teaching communication skills in "child terms" with room for improvement as children grow is groundbreaking in today's society.

Children's communication has eight foundational elements. These include appropriate language, turn-taking, self-awareness, deep thinking, and interaction skills. Others are pausing, standard listening and speaking guidelines, and real-world speaking or listening exercises. Any tasks, games, or activities blending these fundamentals can improve communication skills (Miller, 2019).

Children are encouraged to express their wants through interactive activities. Children are also more inclined to participate in these activities if they perceive them to be entertaining and interesting.

Six Engaging Child Games and Activities

If you're looking for fun ways to impart your child important life skills and lessons, trying these short activities can help.

Identify the object. Many children derive pleasure from playing this game because it improves their description abilities.

Create a hole in a box, making it big enough for a child's hand.

Inform the players that peering through the hole is not allowed.

Put something in the box. Urge each child to touch the item without looking at it.

Encourage each player to make a speculative guess after describing how the object feels.

Display and Tell. Children like giving and receiving gifts. Setting aside time for children to share things with friends can improve their interaction and active listening skills (Miller, 2019).

Ask the players to discuss what they've shared with their classmates.

Emotions Corner. Children who struggle with emotional expression will find this activity interesting.

Create a space for children to express their feelings, providing an emotion printing wheel.

Prepare complementary emojis that children can study or discuss with their peers.

Encourage your kids to share their feelings with you (or with their teachers when in school).

For children who yell when misunderstood or offended, this activity helps them establish trust and compassion.

Turn-Taking. Speaking at different times is like sharing a choice toy. Children must learn this skill.

Color circles are an enjoyable turn-taking exercise for children (Miller, 2019). Each player stands in the circle to speak about a topic.

Suppose yellow is the color children want to use. A child is told to list every yellow item in the class or room. They have 15 seconds to perform this task.

The child will suggest another color for the next player.

After each session, instruct the participants to share two things they learned.

Image-Telling. Provide different pictures for each child. Set a time restriction for the participants and let each player tell stories about the images in their possession.

Children playing this game will be analyzing visual cues and using their interaction skills to relate them to their peers, while other children will be improving their listening abilities.

Complete-the-Kid-Rhyme Tale. Children won't enjoy this activity if they are not familiar with the nursery rhymes being used.

Use entertaining and original methods to assist children in imagining and expressing different nursery rhyme endings.

Have each player contribute to the entire nursery

rhyme tale.

Storytelling helps improve speaking and listening skills in children (Miller, 2019).

Six Communication Games and Exercises for Young Children

A popular "playground game," the telephone also serves as a potent metaphor for explaining miscommunications and the act of transferring information. The remaining games are similarly enjoyable.

Telephone. Invite the class to form a circle. The student sitting next to the teacher will receive one brief topic, sentence, or phrase from the teacher in their ear. Each student will whisper this phrase into the other's ear as they move in a circle around the teacher, who will then compare the original and final sentences.

Emotional Charades. Write out scenarios that might make participants feel something. The scenarios should often involve mild feelings, such as forgetting your lunch, misplacing your phone, becoming the subject of a rumor, being on the bus, or skipping your homework.

The next step is for each student to act out a situation without speaking. Discuss the emotional response once someone has guessed the scenario. The easier a teacher can communicate with a class and bring up perplexing thoughts, the more readily students can verbally articulate their concerns.

Audiobook Interaction. Students can access various interactive books from Scholastic at no cost. The advantage of this interactive learning opportunity is that it helps the student connect between reading and speaking the book's words.

Internet Resources. One website that brings together students from all over the world and provides a forum for learning about creative and effective communication skills is www.creatubbles.com.

Role-Playing. Role-playing is a fantastic technique for developing perspective-taking and empathy. Setting goals for the roles helps steer the children toward words that will better promote cooperation.

For instance, giving students the role of parents or instructors encourages them to utilize their imaginations when coming up with language that adults would use and when considering how it might feel to observe a situation from a perspective other than their own.

The Follow All Instructions Activity. Make a list of thorough directions. READ ALL INSTRUCTIONS FIRST should be the first instruction. IGNORE ALL OTHER INSTRUCTIONS AND WRITE YOUR NAME ON THE TOP OF THIS PAPER should be the last instruction.

Due to this practice, students will learn the value of reading all instructions before starting any project. Additionally, it provides excellent conversation for children of all ages.

Seven Engaging Student Games and Exercises

Children and older pupils can use the games discussed so far, but if you're particularly interested in activities your eight to fourteen-year-olds could do, encourage them to try these entertaining exercises.

Popular Pairs. Romeo and Juliet. Jelly and peanut butter. Ask the participants to make a list of famous pairs they know.

Each player should get a post-it note and write one-half of a popular pair on it.

Other players will walk around the room, identifying the person on a post-it note and asking three questions about them.

After learning about a particularly popular figure, a player then proceeds to locate the person with the other half.

Each player shouldn't reveal themselves until their pair knows who they are.

Best School Features. Many children have negative opinions or views of education, but this skill-building exercise aims to help children identify the positive aspects of their school.

Assign three days for this activity.

Each child uses the first day to state or write the top ten things they love about their school.

Group the participants on the second day — the groups will work together to compile a list of the important features of their school.

After each group has provided their top suggestions for the school, use the third day to make a class-wide list.

Mysterious Self. Other people often say we're weird or secretive. This game encourages self-awareness regarding the things that you find baffling or struggle to understand about yourself.

As part of this exercise, each player will list three unique facts about themselves.

Participants will read the puzzling details to one another in groups of three or four.

Each group will collect the secrets. Later, after reading the fact lists, each group will ask the participants to suggest from whom the facts on their lists come.

Promote a sense of deep respect for these mysteries when organizing this activity for children. Encourage pupils to remember and appreciate one another's differences. Remember that strong trust is frequently built on mutual understanding and respect.

Say No to Fillers. How many children use fillers like *um*, *uh*, *like*, or *so* when interacting with friends, teachers, or caregivers?

You can stop filler phrases when speaking in public or during a conversation by doing this exercise.

Give each child a subject to discuss for two or three minutes. Keep the topic simple and understandable.

The rest of the class will stand throughout the student's speaking period if they hear any of these fillers.

This activity keeps the speaker conscious of their word choice while the class listens.

The entire class stands when these fillers are said — this stuns the speaker and helps them get organized. So, they benefit from exercising caution while choosing or using specific words.

Blindfold game. Use the materials in the classroom to create a barrier course. Divide the pupils into two groups. Encourage the children to cover their eyes.

The groups decide how to transmit instructions while wearing blindfolds and navigating the course from their seats.

Time each group and discuss which form of communication worked best.

Building trust is a key part of this exercise. Children need clear communication skills to complete the course.

Keep the blindfolded learners safe throughout the

lesson—ensure someone stands close to a blindfolded child.

Inspired Understanding. Place two students side by side—while one pupil holds something, the other holds paper and colored pencils.

Without outright identifying the item the first pupil is holding, they must provide a detailed description of the item.

Based on how well the first pupil described the object, the second student must draw the item as best as they can.

Discover It Collectively. This exercise requires a blindfold. Pair the players—one child wears a blindfold while the other doesn't. Their task is to remove particular items from a predetermined circle.

The other student helps their friend wearing a blindfold to find the right item. The game could be disorganized since there are other blindfolded participants.

So, the activity needs coordination, speech recognition, and talking after the activity. For example, how people disregard sound distractions could be a good concluding conversation topic. This makes discussions about listening and management interesting.

Five Nonverbal Communication Games and Activities

Children use both verbal and nonverbal signs when interacting with their peers. These games help teach children conversation skills.

You Stay Quiet. Create groups—five to seven pupils can make a group. Encourage the participants to identify and make a list of nonverbal cues.

Make another smaller group—maybe two or three children in one group. Ask them to provide examples of nonverbal actions.

Encourage the parties to demonstrate these actions while explaining their importance. Participants learn to identify others' nonverbal clues through this practice.

Students should act out one of the nonverbal cues in their groups while the others share or record the cues they notice.

Nonverbal signals may include nodding, smiling, yawning, or frowning. Sitting with arms crossed could also be a nonverbal sign.

Some children might be walking around the room,

tapping their fingers on the table, and resting their chins in their palms or on their knuckles—these are nonverbal pointers.

Ask the players to return later to discuss their findings in small groups.

Identify any instances where a particular nonverbal cue is transmitted to you more strongly than any words by asking the class if they have ever experienced one. They probably have—sharing their personal experience might be a unique lesson for everyone.

Describing Pictures with Writing. This activity encourages creative communication using storytelling and descriptive language.

Hold up someone's photograph—ask the participants to describe in writing what's happening and how people are feeling in the image.

With younger pupils, the teacher can instruct them to illustrate what happens next. This is a fantastic way to convey their creativity and feelings.

Mimes. Prepare a list of questions on particular subjects children can relate to. Group the children to form partnerships.

Pose the topic-related question's response to a pupil through acting.

Encourage another student to make a guess and write down their answer on a sheet of paper.

Motion Sticks. The participants will hold two poles with a pair of fingers and adapt to the poles' movement—a fun and engaging method of learning body language.

Mirrors. Pair up the participants. Assign a leader to each group. Ask a partner to mimic their leader's nonverbal cues and body language.

This exercise helps improve the understanding of body language cues, eye contact, and emotional awareness.

Switch leadership in each group—ask the pupils if they prefer to lead or follow. Ask them why.

Managing emotions requires communication. If your child develops negative emotions, chatting with them helps identify and manage the problem. Introducing engaging social activities into your child's routine may help improve their communication skills. If something is wrong with your child's feelings, be the first to spot it. Teach them to label and manage their emotions. Your child will learn to calm their anger in the next chapter.

Chapter Five:

Calming My Anger

Anger is an emotion that helps you recognize when something is wrong or you feel unpleasant. It is not a bad emotion, but its consequences can be harmful.

Anger can help you by motivating you to do something, warning you to avoid dangerous situations, or speaking up for yourself. It can sometimes have negative consequences. Everything in excess is dangerous.

Similarly, when your anger exceeds normal levels,

and you cannot control it because your anger is controlling you, the effects of anger on you can be dangerous.

It is critical to manage and control anger skillfully and healthily to prevent negative effects on you.

You may have difficulty controlling yourself when angry. You could injure yourself or others.

You may experience severe headaches. Anger increases the likelihood of developing heart and brain diseases, such as heart attack and stroke.

Anger triggers are people, places, situations, or things that cause children to become angry.

Identifying triggers is critical for enabling children to avoid these triggers to prevent anger.

Anger Triggers

Write below the things, events, or people that trigger anger in you.

....

....

....

....

....

....

Where Does It Feel?

Anger can be felt in various body parts, including the head and chest.

Anger is commonly felt in the head as a headache, in the chest as pressure or pain, and in the heart as a burning sensation or striking feeling.

Identifying the body parts where anger is felt and taking the necessary precautions to avoid these effects can help with anger bursts.

Anger occurs on purpose and is not harmful in many ways, but if it persists and begins to control an individual, it can have a negative impact.

In the picture below, mark the body parts affected when you get angry. For example, mark the head region in the picture below if you get a headache when you get angry.

How I Feel When I'm Angry

When angry, I feel: (Tick inside the box what you usually feel)

- Irritated

- Sad

- Tense

- Anxious

- Full of negative thoughts.

    Others……………………..

What Happens to My Body When I'm Angry?

- I have a lot of energy and need to do something or fix something.

- I am unable to control myself.

- My muscles tense.

- I clench my fist.

- My jaw muscles tighten.

- I frown.

- My breathing becomes fast and agitated.

- My heart rate is extremely rapid.

- My face may turn red.

- My ears are burning.

- I feel like screaming.

- My voice changes, becoming louder and faster or even completely silent.

- My face also tells me I'm angry:

- My brows constrict and fall.

- My pupils contract and narrow.

- My lips tighten and contract.

- My nostrils are dilated.

It's Dangerous to Let Your Anger Run Wild

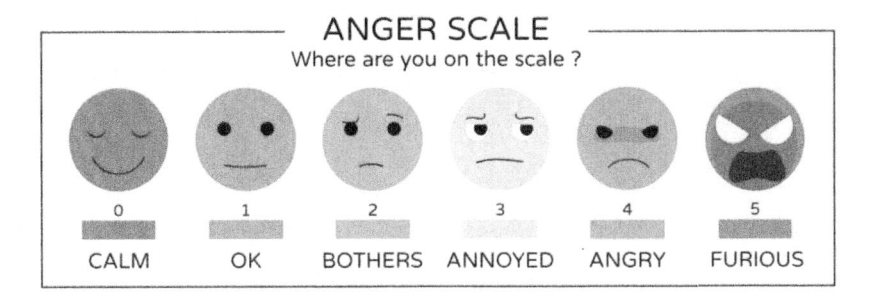

ANGER SCALE
Where are you on the scale?

0	1	2	3	4	5
CALM	OK	BOTHERS	ANNOYED	ANGRY	FURIOUS

You hurt yourself when you allow your anger to go wild. Read this story:

A snake invaded a carpenter's workshop when they were away. The snake hoped it would find food in the carpenter's place because it was hungry. It moved slowly back and forth across the space, ran into an ax, and got injured.

Being furious, the snake attacked the ax but bled more. So, the snake said, *I'm going to choke and kill this useless ax by wrapping around it.*

The snake was dead when the carpenter got to his workplace the following morning.

If you're a parent, your two-year-olds may develop tempers since tantrums are common in their age group (Rouse, n.d.). But, if your child experiences frequent outbursts as they approach school age, it could indicate that they struggle with emotional self-regulation.

If your child is five years or older and still suffers from tempers, they may require assistance in learning to regulate their feelings or actions. Self-regulation, the ability to control emotions and actions, helps children withstand intensely emotional responses and distressing situations. It involves regaining control of their emotions when they become unhappy and adjusting to altered expectations.

If your children acquire self-regulation skills, they can control their anger without losing control. It is a set of abilities that allows children to control their behavior to achieve a goal despite the instability of the outside environment and their own emotions (Rouse, n.d.).

Some children struggle more naturally with self-control. Parents who constantly step in to address issues or calm their children often prevent them from learning these skills. Children learn to self-regulate on their own. Avoiding challenging circumstances is not the answer either; instead, focus on guiding your children through challenging circumstances.

If your children struggle to implement assignments, it can be beneficial to help them divide a task into smaller, more manageable pieces. For example, if they struggle to brush their teeth, encourage them to start by placing toothpaste on their brush. When they succeed, praise them and gradually introduce more steps.

Encourage children who misbehave to take their time and think—this helps them reflect and question the motive behind their behaviors and also think about how to address the situation.

Practicing mindfulness benefits self-regulation. Mindful children focus more on the present, not the past or future.

As a parent, applying these tips may prevent your kid's anger from going wild.

Do Runs. Make a quick trip when you don't need to do any significant shopping, especially when your child acts impulsively.

Tell your child to walk without touching anything. They receive points toward a certain objective each time they succeed.

Parents frequently experience failure the first time when attempting to develop their children's skills, but consistency is important. Starting at a level suitable for your child is also crucial.

Don't give up! Simplifying the task or making it more manageable and gradually increasing your child's independence will help their progress. Suppose your child has trouble cleaning their teeth. Encourage them to put toothpaste on the brush and offer rewards when they succeed.

Tag emotions. Using words like *unhappy*, *frustrated*, or *mad* to describe feelings helps children develop self-awareness (SDK First, n.d.). When describing emotions to young children, it may be helpful to use visual images like faces and numbers.

Teach your children to deal with emotions. Children act out when struggling to understand or express their feelings. For example, a child who cannot express their anger verbally may try to act it out. Similarly, if a child cannot express their sadness, they act out to attract attention (Morin, 2021).

Introducing feeling words like *glad, shocked, sad,* or *angry* to children will assist them to identify and group their emotions.

Expressions such as *"It seems like you're angry"* or *"You look happy now"* can help children learn their feelings.

Teaching your children emotional words or phrases like *frustrated, let down, lonely,* and *anxious* will help them understand and express their feelings more.

Develop a calm-down program. Show your children how to handle anger. Instead of acting out, creating a *calming corner* may help. Your child can head straight to this corner to relax when they're angry (Morin, 2021).

Suggesting coloring or reading (like other calming activities) may help your children relax and feel better. You may even provide a relaxation kit in the *calming corner*. The kit may contain crayons, stickers, coloring books, or your kid's choice (favorite) toys.

If a child looks upset, telling them to grab their calm-down kit encourages them to take charge of their calming-down program.

Cultivate anger management skills. Teaching practical methods to manage anger is one of the finest ways to support a furious child. For example, when a child is angry, taking deep breaths might help them feel better physically and mentally. Also, taking a brief walk or repeating a helpful phrase like *I know how I feel, and I can manage it,* or *I will feel better once I get into my calming corner* may help.

Avoid violent media. Exposing your child to violent video games or TV shows may worsen their aggressive behavior (if they already exhibit it). Instead, expose children to books, games, and television shows that serve as good role models for effective dispute resolution (Morin, 2021).

Practice relaxation techniques. Being calm and upset at the same time is nearly impossible. You can teach relaxation in many ways—for example; you can utilize personal cues like images, words, or phrases when faced with a challenging circumstance.

Children may enjoy visualizing a favorite song or narrative. You can introduce other strategies, such as breathing, visualization, or meditation.

Teach empathy. Encourage your children to consider other people's views—even children know when someone else is upset or furious. If your child doesn't want to discuss their emotions, involving a beloved book character may help (Morin, 2021).

Tell children to tolerate one another. Even nice individuals can occasionally act badly. Someone who has lost their anger before can still change. Make your children understand that their actions won't be held against them forever.

Exercises for Calming Anger

Breathing

You are probably thinking, "Breathing? Really? I breathe all the time! And that has never helped my anger!"

It is true—you do breathe all the time! Breathing is something our bodies do automatically. We don't even need to think about it. But did you know that not every breath is the same? Don't believe it? Let's practice!

Fast Breathing

Set a timer for twenty seconds, or ask a grown-up to set one for you. When the timer starts, breathe in and out as fast as possible. Keep going until the timer rings. Your breathing might sound a lot like a dog panting fast.

How was that? The twenty seconds probably felt like a long time! How does your body feel now? Do you feel calm and relaxed? Or is your heart beating super fast? Is your belly a little tired?

Slow Breathing

Now, try breathing in and out slowly. There are several approaches to doing this.

You can take a deep breath in as you count one-two-three-four. Then, blow it out as you count one-two-three-four.

You can also hold your hands together, and when you breathe out, move them apart like a balloon is blowing up. When the balloon is full, take a long, deep breath in as you bring your hands together to make the balloon flat again.

Make sure to do at least five in-and-out breaths in a row.

How was that? Your heart is probably beating nicely and slowly now. Different body parts (like your stomach, arms, and legs) might feel pretty relaxed.

Try doing this activity when you feel anger start to build in your body. Take five deep breaths before you decide what you want to do with your anger.

Imaginary Special Place

We discussed before how if we think positive thoughts, we will start to feel better. When we use our imagination to think about something fun, like a birthday party or a trip to Disneyland, we can start to feel better.

Another way we can feel better is to create a special place in our minds full of happy thoughts and memories. When we think about this place, we feel better.

For this activity, think about five happy memories or five things you love. Then, using a piece of paper, create a picture that collects all five objects or memories in a single location.

Here are five examples of happy memories or objects:

A birthday party

A trip to the beach

Playing games with a friend

A pet cat

A favorite superhero

Spaghetti Dance and Sauce

Moving our bodies in a silly and safe way is a great way to get the anger out. For this activity, there are two parts.

Part 1: Spaghetti Arms and Legs Dance

Make sure there is space around you so you will not get hurt. Then, pretend your arms and legs have turned into spaghetti noodles! Dance around with your arms and legs loose and wiggly like cooked spaghetti. Then, change your arms and legs into uncooked spaghetti, which is straight and hard. Do this for one to three minutes or until you are tired.

Part 2: Sauce It Up!

After you have done the spaghetti dance, drop to the ground. Imagine your spaghetti arms and legs are now covered with tomato sauce. As you lie on the ground, pretend to slurp up the spaghetti and the sauce slowly. Breathe slowly, in and out.

How was that? Did you have fun being spaghetti? Do you feel calmer now?

Distraction

A fast way to deal with our anger is to do something we like or something that distracts us (aka, it shifts our thoughts to more neutral or positive ones). We don't want this to become our only tool to help us with the anger monster. But as you work on your anger, distracting yourself can help you move away from anger quickly.

There are many ways to distract yourself. Here are three simple ones.

Ball Toss

This activity is just like it sounds. Get a ball and toss it back and forth with a grown-up, sibling, or friend. Focus on trying to catch it each time without dropping it. Try throwing the ball with your other hand, behind your back, or between your legs. Be creative!

21 Questions

For this game, one person picks a person, place, or thing. They could pick a superhero, hospital, or cheetah. Then, the other person asks simple yes-or-no questions. Questions could be: Is it a person? Is it an animal? Have I seen it before?

I Spy

For this activity, one person chooses something that both of you can see in the place where you are. (For example, if you are in a classroom, it would be anything you could see in the classroom or through the window that won't move out of sight). Then, the person says something about what they see, like, "I see something green." Now the other person tries to guess what the thing is by asking questions. Questions could be, "Is it one of the books on the shelf? Is it outside? Is it a tree?"

Distracting yourself when angry helps your body change from feeling stressed to calm. Later, when you are back to feeling calm, you can think more about what happened to make you angry. Then, you can plan to do something different in the future so the anger doesn't happen.

STOPP

STOPP, a method that observes how people inhale and exhale, can help children manage intense feelings under pressure (Clear View, n.d.).

What concerns or physical feelings do you have?

Here's how to use *STOPP*.

Say stop. Telling yourself to stop when worried (or your body responds to a stressor) helps pause the reaction. The earlier you say this, the better.

Breathe. Taking a few deeper, slower breaths can calm the bodily response to emotion and adrenaline, the anxiety-releasing body hormone (Clear View, n.d.). You can refresh your brain and think sensibly by focusing on your breathing and freeing your mind from angry thoughts and feelings.

Observe. We are aware of our thoughts, physical feelings, and impulsive urges. We can observe the cycle of our concern and anger.

Noticing these thoughts and emotions helps us to avoid them.

Adopt an objective viewpoint. Changing one's thinking is STOPP's objective. Disturbing ideas are lessened when someone takes a step back from emotional situations and focuses on the wider picture. You can achieve this by analyzing your thoughts.

Practice what's more effective for you.

Nature Play

Getting closer to nature helps increase awareness and boost mindfulness. Your children will enjoy nature if you organize a family day in a local park or rural area. Practicing these activities with your children can help them prevent emotional problems.

Breathe in, paying attention to your immediate environment — what sounds can you hear? What's the loudest or quietest sound you can hear?

Breathe out, moving or walking silently.

Emotions Jenga

Emotions Jenga or *Therapy Jenga* is an interesting game children use to communicate their feelings and experiences

(Childhood 101, n.d.). With a permanent marker, players create words that illustrate certain emotions on wood blocks.

The participants will arrange the blocks after writing their feelings on them. Setting things up involves two methods—facing or backing the words.

Ask your child to hang the blocks if they are worried that they are unable to read the few hidden words on the blocks—this helps them read and understand the words.

Emotions Jenga has two versions. One method is to explain the word you choose before writing it—young children without a strong emotional wordbook will enjoy playing this game this way.

In the second method, the player must describe a time or event in their life when they had a particular feeling. You can analyze further by urging your children to express their feelings (happy and sad moments).

Keep the words clear and avoid using language that is too advanced or hard to understand, especially with children who are new to this and still feel uncomfortable discussing their emotions.

Thoughtful Journal

Journaling offers a straightforward way to cultivate mindfulness and could be a great chance for children to develop their writing skills, jotting their best memories and ideas.

Here are a few clever journaling questions for children.

What experiences stick in your mind?

Have you had a surprising event lately? What was it?

Which three things are you most appreciative of in your life?

Share your recent mistakes and the lessons they taught you.

What one item helps you handle anxiety?

Body Scan Yoga

The body scan is an important mindfulness meditation for children. It helps prevent pain, stress, and other discomforts and also creates a stronger sense of emotion and self-awareness in children (Raypole, 2022).

Follow these steps to practice body scan meditation.

Lie or sit effortlessly, extending your limbs.

Focus on your breath and close your eyes. Inhale and exhale, paying attention to how your lungs fill and empty air.

Continue inhaling and exhaling slowly, stretching your right hand, left foot, or other body parts.

Be aware of painful feelings you may experience — spend between one and three minutes noting these emotions. If you feel furious, don't blame yourself.

Picture the painful feelings departing from your body as you inhale and exhale.

Use Puppets and Stories

Anger is a negative emotion, and experiencing it may be inappropriate. However, no emotion is incorrect because each one serves a purpose. Use puppets to help your child express their anger if they are uncomfortable talking about it. You can also give their rage an exciting name, such as "anger monster," and it will help children become more comfortable with the concept of anger and express their emotions more effectively. Tales may also educate kids on how to face challenges. Learning about people might motivate children to aspire and benefit from them. Stories can also teach children how to deal with difficult situations.

Introduce the 1+3+10 Activity

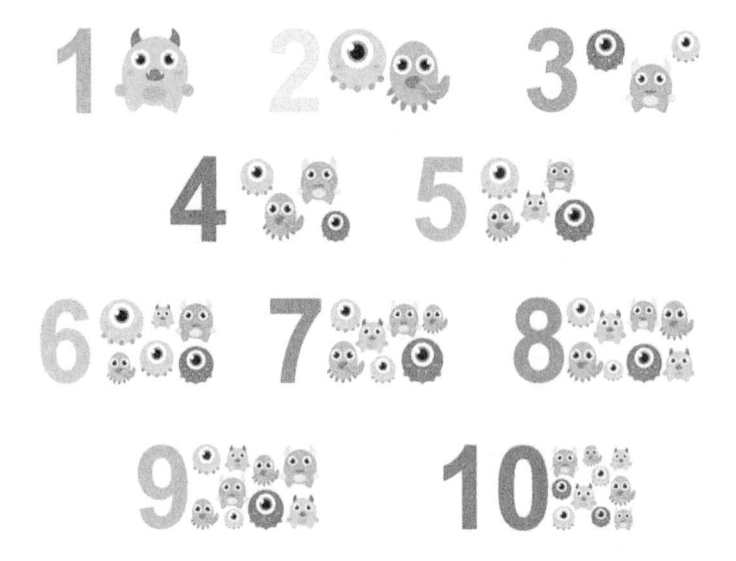

1 🐲 2 🐙 3 👾
4 🐙 5 👾
6 👾 7 🐙 8 👾
9 👾   10 👾

The first step is to pause and remind themselves to remain calm.

The child should then take three slow, deep breaths.

The child should count to ten.

Repeating the 1+3+10 activity will help the child become calm and control their anger.

Draw a Picture

Some children may not be able to express themselves verbally, but they can express themselves through drawing.

Drawing allows them to unwind and relax.

If your children enjoy drawing, encourage them to use it as an outlet for their frustration.

The Mindfulness Jar

Mindfulness jars—the tools helping children calm and self-conscious when worried—are portable, easy-to-use containers filled with water and glitter (Hudson Therapy, 2019).

You'll need a container, transparent glue, heated water, and glitter to make a mindful jar for your children.

These steps will guide you to make one for your children right away.

Put the transparent glue in the container, ensuring that the container's bottom is covered. More glue means a longer time for glitter to settle.

Add glitter. Fill the container with water to dissolve the glue.

Include favorite quotes or decorations.

Consider the container in its motionless state — it should have a clear top while the glitter sits at the container's bottom, symbolizing children's state of mind when free or happy (Hudson Therapy, 2019).

Shaking the container makes the glitter whirl or spin about, showing people's feelings when furious, stressed, or worried.

View the glitter — the three colors depict our mood, opinions, and actions. Children lose all these when furious or acting out.

Playing the mindfulness jar game helps children learn how emotions affect decisions and actions. Children may also develop mindfulness skills by focusing on the furious glitter when shaking the container.

Helping children discover their triggers is crucial to anger management. When your child gets furious, learning what's causing their emotional distress can help. Cooperate with your child to work out the appropriate anger-management strategies. Like anger, calming anxiety is key, and that's what you will learn in the next chapter.

Chapter Six:
Calming My Anxiety

Do you wonder if worries are normal? Or what worries even are? The first step in learning how to handle worries is to understand them. Understanding what worries are, and knowing what your worries are, will help you recognize when it's happening. When you can recognize worry, you'll be able to know when it's time to use the skills you learn in this chapter.

What Are Worries?

Maybe you've been told, "You worry too much!" But what exactly are worries? Worry is a type of thought (Goldstein, 2016). Worry thoughts are usually about something bad happening that hasn't happened yet, and might not ever happen but that you think could happen. Maybe you even think it WILL happen. A lot of times, worry thoughts start with "What if . . . ?"

What if I get sick?

What if I fail that test?

What if people laugh at me?

A lot of children worry about things like getting hurt, making mistakes, or people getting mad at them. Worries can be about any bad thing you think could happen. These types of thoughts make people feel anxious, nervous, or scared.

Even though worries often start with "what if," the question isn't what children are really worried about. It's the answer to the "what if?" question that makes them feel anxious. And our imaginations sure can come up with all kinds of scary answers that can seem very convincing. Even though they come from your brain, it can feel like worries have a mind of their own (NHS, n.d.).

It can help to think of worries as coming from outside of you. Some people compare worries to a bug buzzing around their heads, like a pest that just won't go away. Some people think about worries like they're a scary noise coming from behind a closed door—they may feel afraid of what's on the other side, but when they are brave enough to open the door, they see it was just a trick, and there was nothing to be afraid of after all.

Here's another way to think about worries. Have you ever known someone who exaggerated things a lot? Maybe they told you something easy to believe, like they had a birthday party, but then added details that made it hard to believe, like they had a thousand guests and a hundred-foot-tall cake that everyone climbed before taking rides on a real-life unicorn.

A friend like this might try hard to convince you that their stories are true and even get mad at you for not believing them. They might even try to get you to make decisions based on their false information.

If this friend seemed to care about you and was helpful, you might want to keep them around. But would you trust everything they told you, knowing they exaggerated so much? Do you think you would believe everything this friend said?

Probably not. You'd likely want to do some investigating yourself before deciding which things to believe (like they had a party with guests and cake and had fun) and which things to ignore (there were a thousand guests, a cake so big people could climb it, and a mythical creature at the party).

Worry is a lot like this friend. Sometimes, it wants what's best for you and may even give you helpful or important information, but it exaggerates A LOT. You might even want to give your worried friend a name, like "Worrying Wally" or "Exaggerating Edna."

Sometimes, children know what their thoughts are, and sometimes, their worry is more like a feeling, like being scared or nervous or just not wanting to do something. If you're one of those children who feel scared but don't know why it's okay. The exercises in this chapter can help you figure out what's bothering you. It might be hard to think about sometimes, but I know you can do it.

Where Do My Worries Come From?

Even though worry can be normal and helpful, it doesn't feel good. You may wonder why you have these problems when other children don't seem to. You might never know exactly where your anxiety comes from. This chapter will give you some ideas.

Do any of your family members feel anxious a lot? People don't always say when they're worried or anxious, but sometimes, you can tell by how they act if you pay close attention. Maybe you have a parent who is always asking you if you're sure you've done all your homework (even though you always do) or an aunt or uncle who cleans a lot or is always double-checking to make sure they turned off the stove and locked all the doors or a grandparent who is afraid to fly. One thing we know is that anxiety often runs in families. This means that if one person in a family has anxiety or worries a lot, they are more likely to have relatives who also feel that way.

Another possible reason some children might worry more is that there can be differences in the brains and bodies of people who get anxious easily. They might be more sensitive to small changes in how their bodies feel (kind of like a smoke alarm that goes off every time someone cooks food instead of only when there's a fire), and it might take their bodies longer to calm down and get back to their normal level.

External forces can make a child feel more worried or anxious. For example, they might see other people acting scared or anxious about things and can learn to be afraid of them, too. Or they might have something stressful happen, like moving, their parents divorcing, or other big life changes, or they might feel pressure to do many things or perform well.

Some children start to feel anxious after something that feels really bad or scary happens to them. Getting sick or hurt, being in an accident or a bad storm, being treated unfairly, or having someone you love get hurt or die is really upsetting. Some children worry about those things happening again, making them feel anxious anytime something reminds them of that scary event.

There are times when children feel some other feeling, but they don't realize it; instead, they feel anxious. This is called a hidden emotion, and it happens when something is bothering you that you think you should be okay with, so you hide the fact that it's bothering you from everyone — even yourself! This happens a lot to children who are really nice and don't want to upset anyone, so their brains hide their real feelings, and they only realize they feel anxious.

It is apparent that there are several sources of concern, and the solution will change for each individual. It may be that your worry comes from one or a combination of several of these things or even someplace else. It may feel helpful to know where your worry or anxiety comes from, but it's okay if you don't know exactly what's causing it; you can still learn to feel better!

Where Do I Feel My Anxiety?

Write or draw your physical sensations on the following picture where they happen on your body. Here is a handful of concepts, but you can add your own:

Heart beating fast or hard

Upset stomach

Sweating

Headache

Stomachache

Butterflies in stomach

Tense muscles

Shaking

Sweating

Trouble focusing

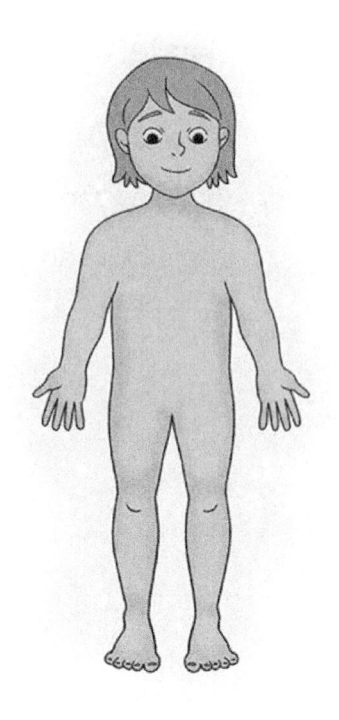

How Do I Calm My Anxiety

If you're stressed or worried, practicing these activities may ease your condition.

Stress balls. Encouraging children to make stress balls can improve their mental health. Giving them something to concentrate on will make them feel more at ease, and they will leave with a useful tool that will help them relax their body and mind when under stress or anxiety (Meraki Lane, n.d.).

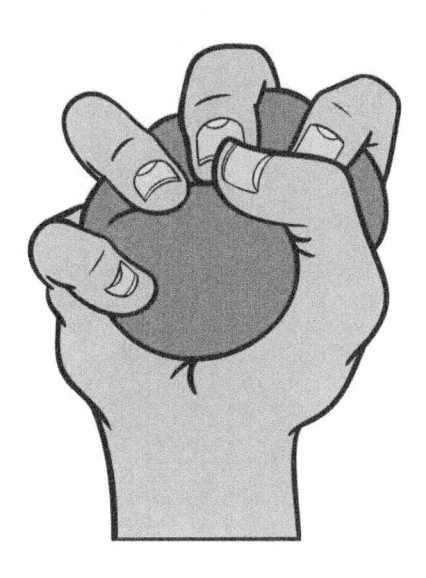

All you need to make your stress ball is a funnel, balloons, and a choice of filling materials—rice and wheat work fine. Using many balloons helps prevent the mess following ruptured stress balls.

Feelings Thermometer. Teaching children how their ideas and feelings affect their conduct is the goal of mind-behavioral therapy. So, making a feelings thermometer tops the list of things to consider when aiming for cognitive behavioral therapy exercises for children.

ANGER THERMOMETER

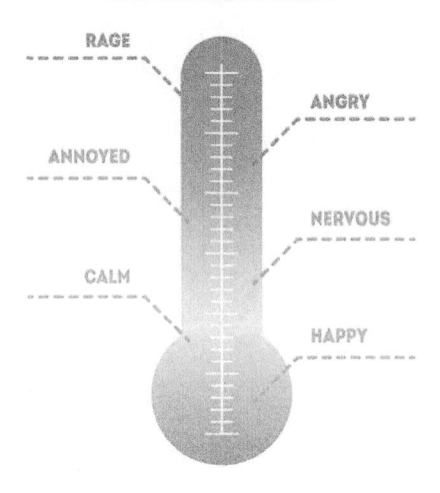

- RAGE
- ANGRY
- ANNOYED
- NERVOUS
- CALM
- HAPPY

With this activity, children can learn the fundamentals of emotion and discover the varying degrees of each feeling.

A feelings thermometer is an excellent picture that parents can provide for their children to boost their emotional awareness, help them understand the connection between their thoughts, behaviors, and feelings, and teach them self-regulation skills (Meraki Lane, n.d.).

Calm-down jars. Exposing children to calm-down jars may improve their mental behavior. These jars are simple to build and may be very calming since they can reduce anxiety and aid anger management.

As a child arranges their thoughts on the calm-down

jar, shakes it, and sees the contents settle, their mind learns to focus. The idea is that as the contents of the calm-down jar drop, your child's heart rate will regulate, allowing them to develop control over their emotions.

Mindful breathing. Our breathing patterns vary when scared or worried—we breathe rapid breaths, which might worsen our present worrying state.

There are many strategies caregivers can use to practice mindful breathing with children, which is a terrific skill to learn when emotions control their bodies. For example, the BBT (bubble-blowing technique) teaches children mindfulness (Meraki Lane, n.d.).

Give children a tiny plastic soap bubble wand and container, and tell them to practice blowing bubbles. They'll learn that blowing too forcefully or rapidly causes the bubble to break before it has a chance to form. They can produce a flawless bubble by blowing slowly and gently.

Encourage the players to rehearse the process with real bubbles before taking away the soap and asking them to use their imaginations.

Hissing Breath is another engaging mindful exercise for older children—it entails inhaling through the nose and exhaling with a long hissing sound via the mouth. Teach children that the longer they can maintain a hissing sound, the better their respiratory control.

Don't go bananas. Try this activity when looking for a kid-friendly game with an easy setup process. It helps children control the five major emotions—jealousy, anger, fear, sadness, and anxiety. Practice this exercise often to support your child's mental development (Meraki Lane, n.d.).

If a child engages in this activity, it helps them identify the causes of these emotions, how to respond to them, and how they may impact their mental processes.

Optimistic mantra bracelet. This activity is a fun way to encourage children to develop positive thinking and learn the mantras relating to them.

Ask them about their top concerns first, then work with them to create three or four mantras (like I'm safe or I will overcome my concerns) they can say to themselves under pressure.

Assign each phrase to a different colored bead. Instruct the children to thread them all together onto a pipe cleaner and wear it as a wristband reminder to breathe and think positively every day.

Worry box. Children may develop a sense of helplessness when controlling their worried thoughts. They won't stop talking about a particular subject or issue they lack sufficient time to address. Children with anxiety problems will benefit from participating in the worry box activity (Meraki Lane, n.d.).

Use markers, mod podge, glitter, stickers, and choice craft supplies to make a customized box for your children. As they build their box, tell them that's where they'll store their worries until they have time to deal with them.

Children can put their worries in the box after writing them down. Parents can help their children feel like they have some control over their anxieties by setting aside time in their day to talk about them. They can discard the piece of paper once they no longer have to address a particular fear in the box.

Belly Butterflies. Using this game to encourage children to discuss their fears or worries is a sweet way to improve their mental well-being.

Trace a kid's head and torso on a sizable piece of oak wood, drawing and cutting out various-sized butterflies and then arranging them in a pattern (Meraki Lane, n.d.).

Talk to each participant about the bodily symptoms of worry (like the stomach butterflies people feel).

With different sizes for large and minor anxieties, ask children to write down various worries they have.

Tell the children how to catch the butterflies and stay calm. Record your findings.

Journaling. Many children struggle to vocally express themselves or lack a parent or other close confidant with whom they may talk about their emotions.

Tell children they can choose another form of expression if talking about their stress or worries makes them feel uncomfortable. Encourage them to keep a notebook and let them decorate it with markers, stickers, or even magazine cutouts of encouraging words or images.

Calming anxiety requires understanding the triggers; if your child worries a lot, asking them what's causing the concerns can help. Being your child's best friend encourages them to share their problems with you. Your child will learn to calm their stress in the next chapter.

Chapter Seven:

Calming My Stress

Any unusual event can cause children stress. Anything that makes children worried is the cause of stress in them. When children feel fear or pressure in their minds, they become stressed, which impacts their health and body. Stress can make children dull, shy, aggressive, hyper, and mentally and physically sick. There are different causes behind each stress, and different children can get stressed differently. One thing causing stress for one child may not be the cause for the other, so there is no set pattern for this feeling.

Stress is not always bad. It can be good in some cases. For example, if a child feels pressured to complete a task and wants to get the prize announced by the teacher or parent, it will help them complete the task as required. In addition, intelligent and intellectual students work hard while preparing for an exam, but thinking about the paper can make them stressed. When they put their efforts into the exam and do their best, they can feel stressed while collecting their graded exam.

However, bad stress is harder to handle. Any bad happening can cause this stress, leading to mental and physical medical problems in children. A child can feel such stress when they see something that can make them scared, unsafe, panic, upset, or can disrupt their routine. Parents' relationships, teachers' harshness, class fights, parents' sickness, and many other reasons can cause bad stress in the children. The main thing is finding the cause of stress; when you recognize it in your kid, you can easily cope. Elimination of the things causing bad stress can easily manage the feeling. Parents and guardians must work closely with the children to permanently solve the issue.

What is Stress?

You've probably heard an adult express their stress. What does this imply? Stress is how our bodies react to overwhelming or frightening situations (World Health Organization, 2021). Did you know that stress isn't just a problem for adults? That's correct! Children can experience stress as well. Stress can be caused by too much homework or something more serious, such as losing a loved one. We do not, unfortunately, live in a stress-free world. But there is some good news! You can learn how to manage stress to get through difficult times more easily.

What Causes Stress?

You can find stress anywhere. Knowing what causes you stress can assist you in dealing with that stress. A trigger is something that causes stress. Is your trigger a sibling who occasionally drives you insane? Perhaps, you are concerned about Thursday night because you have a big test on Friday. Maybe loud noises stress you out.

Knowing your stress triggers can help you manage them (Dolgoff, 2020). If your younger brother bothers you and you're tired from school, try to avoid him until you're rested. A little bit of studying each night for your test on Friday might help you relax on Thursday night. Also, if loud noises bother you, do not attend a Fourth of July fireworks display!

What Stresses You Out?

Consider a situation that has caused you stress. Perhaps, you were anxious before a big test or presentation, or perhaps, a beloved family pet died. Consider the following questions in light of this particular incident.

Make a list of the things that stress you out and rate them out of ten (ten being the most stressful situation).

………………………………………………………….

How do you react to these stressful situations? For example, does your stomach become upset, are you usually sad, and so on?

………………………………………………………….

How long do you feel stressed? For example, a short period, an entire day, or multiple days, etc.

………………………………………………………….

Do you take any steps to alleviate the stress? If yes, what do you do in that case?

………………………………………………………….

Stress Relief Activities and Exercises for Children

Do many adults wish they were children when stress strikes? Are they aware that children also experience stress? For example, schoolchildren suffer from jealousy, presentation anxiety, and the concern of losing a friend.

Sometimes, they panic when unable to complete their homework. Today's youth face higher stress levels than their parents did as children (Wow Parenting, n.d.). The level of competitiveness back then wasn't high enough, nor were the problems, either.

Each child has a unique set of stressful trigger factors; they respond uniquely to each event and also have different ways of expressing their stress.

Some cry, while others swallow their stress and display anger later. These kid-friendly activities will aid your children in resolving stressful situations.

Meditation supports inner peace, mindfulness, and stability. It relaxes the body and mind. Many meditation types children can try come with different benefits. For example, engaging in meditation reduces stress.

Proper meditation involves these steps:

Sit on a comfy chair, closing your eyes.

Inhale deeply for two or three seconds.

Exhale gently for two or three seconds.

Music calms people's minds and helps them defeat their problems. Although each person has their musical preferences, music helps people enter a peaceful space. You can create a healthy mood at home by playing relaxing music. For example, chirping birds or running water sounds may help reduce stress in children.

Nature stroll is calming and refreshing. Go for a walk with your children in local gardens with beautiful plants and trees. Plants energize our souls; even medical experts recommend using plants and greens to calm our eyes (Contentment Questing, n.d.). Your child's stress and worries will decrease after a walk outdoors. They will feel refreshed and ready to resume their task.

Touching, like giving a warm embrace, makes children feel loved and cherished. The first ever sensation of security a child feels is their parent's touch. They will identify with it and feel comforted by it.

Hug your child every morning and evening. This will help you and your child have a stronger relationship.

Playing with pets is among the best activities to do with children. Buy your child a pet—a rabbit, dog, cat, or anything you and your child like. If you're not buying a pet, allowing your child to visit their pet-owning friends can be a great idea.

Depending on their age, instruct your child to care for their pets. A child's capacity to think about others and view things from a different perspective improves when they are given responsibility.

Children quickly forget their worries when playing with pets.

Fun brain teasers, like solving puzzles, help develop a child's brain. As children solve these riddles, they lose all memory of previous worries.

Yoga, a mind-body exercise promoting calmness and discipline, stretches a child's muscles and awakens their senses. Practicing yoga 30 minutes daily helps reduce stress (Johns Hopkins, n.d.).

Gardening is an engaging child activity. Take your child shopping so they can buy some seeds, mud, and a pot. Children are naturally calm, so having to cultivate a tree on their own is a new experience for them.

Plants teach vital skills everyone needs to learn, such as patience.

DIY projects help children discover their creativity and ability. Engaging in these projects enables children to focus on knowing more about themselves.

There are many project ideas for children — they can create anything they love, including ceramics, pencil holders, dream catchers, and wall decors. Children enjoy crafting, so give your child colorful sheets, safety scissors, and glue. They will design beautiful objects.

Baking involves making cake, cookies, and other delicious treats. Children will enjoy helping you bake when in the kitchen. Ask them to cover a cake with chocolate chips or knead the dough. They can release stress using their energy to knead the bread.

Be ready to talk. Sometimes, a child has something to tell their caregivers. What prevents them from sharing is the worry that their parents will punish them for acting foolish. In other words, they want to avoid blame.

Although this isn't a casual and fun pastime, creating strong bonds with children is vital. Gently approach your children and reassure them that they won't be blamed or punished. Children need to hear from their parents that they are right there to assist them.

Children are capable of understanding what others want or anticipate from them but cannot determine proper action when facing difficult situations — talking with children is helpful in these moments.

Journaling is a beneficial stress-relieving hobby for

children. Learning to write freely and resolve difficulties on paper can help improve someone's life.

Exposing children to journaling prompts/themes may be beneficial.

- Gratitude is a five-minute journal that creates space for children to write out their thoughts daily. Completing it also requires less time. A gratitude journal teaches children to start and end each day with happy feelings. You may help your kid's mental well-being as parents by urging them to pay attention to the good aspects of their lives.

- Mom and Child is a notebook that strengthens kid-parent relationships. It teaches the importance of regular stress management. Caregivers and their children fill this journal jointly.

- A Fill-in journal is perfect for children without the writing skills to create long diary entries. If your child is young or has problems focusing for extended periods, a fill-in journal would be a good option for them. It includes spaces for children to write their likes and dislikes.

- Scrapbook is a fantastic activity for art-loving children. It gives children a creative outlet and a place to gather and think back on their favorite experiences as they develop, which can be quite peaceful and healing.

  Beginners will probably need a scrapbook kit to get going, but as your child gets older, you may let them pick out a notebook and some gel pens and then observe as they use additional supplies you already have at home.

- Prompts journal is beneficial for older children with tons of feelings and concerns—they can write their ideas in this blank notebook daily. Consider purchasing a diary with a lock for your child to enhance their privacy.

Straw painting is a stress-relieving activity that gets children to focus on their breathing. Inhaling deeply helps a child return to a peaceful state (Wow Parenting, n.d.). A fantastic approach to do this is to create masterpieces of straw painting with your children.

Apply diluted watercolor paints to a piece of paper and instruct your child to smear the paint with a straw by blowing air through it.

Art therapy helps children feel less worried and express their thoughts, including everything they've faced. The stress in children's hearts and minds will be released if they have a safe environment to express their feelings through art therapy.

Art therapy may improve a child's mental and physical health. Coloring, writing, and journaling are just a few of the artistic activities that are included in art therapy.

Although it can be challenging for children to express themselves freely, art therapy may help them feel less disturbed or worried. They can express their secret feelings through their artistic work.

Components of Children's Art Therapy

Artists from the past and the present have long used craft as a coping tool for stress. Children can use these therapy parts to calm or reduce anxiety.

Sculpting. According to published findings, kids who use expressive arts experience happy and less stressful outcomes. The creative phase of sculpting helps children connect with their emotions.

Children can create sculptures at home by enrolling in online classes. They can also create sculptures in groups where several people can work together at once.

Doodling may lessen the impact of stress on children. The rhythmic and repeated action used when a child draws helps calm their body and mind. Drawing helps manage anxiety and relieve tension. When a child doodles, they focus mainly on the task at hand while their brain prioritizes completion above diversion.

A child creates random shapes, lines, or faces when doodling, allowing them to focus on self-discovery.

Drawing, as a form of art therapy, helps reduce tension and anxiety in children.

Collage-making is suitable for children wanting (or needing) to be alone. Collage-making helps children understand their inner personalities. They can create collages without sketching or painting. For example, a child can make a fanciful scene by cutting out different photos from magazines or newspapers and gluing them together.

Socially isolated children or those having trouble building relationships (or making friends) may enjoy this art therapy technique.

Art journaling is especially effective when expressing feelings. When stressed or unwilling to face the outside world, art journaling enables children to make their visual story versions. It also helps improve children's writing skills.

Engaging in this activity helps promote children's creativity and freedom—they can combine text and images to effectively convey a topic.

Painting can help children reduce stress. Painting assists children in expressing their emotions and situations.

Mandala art, which depicts the cosmos and sets spiritual standards, helps relieve tension and anxiety. Children frequently use mandalas to express their inner selves through colors because of their healing and symbolic properties. Making mandalas is a soul-healing ritual—it inspires and directs (Wow Parenting, n.d.).

If your child looks dull, shy, aggressive, or sick, they may be experiencing stressful situations. Telling your child how you manage stress will help them to handle theirs. In the next chapter, you'll see how people feel emotions.

Chapter Eight:

Other People Feel Emotions, Too

"But I don't want to!"

Have you ever said this to an adult, and they said, "You're right. You can do whatever you want!" Probably not, right? It is hard to hear, but no one, not even adults, gets to do everything they want all the time. When the adults around you say "no" or "not now," that is okay, even if it doesn't feel good. They are teaching you about empathy. Empathy means that you can understand and share the feelings of others. Have you ever hoped that others would understand you better?

"Why does my room need to be cleaned? What's the big deal?" Fighting all the time is exhausting! Showing kindness and compassion to others helps us to be heard. When we feel like people hear and understand us, we don't need to fight all the time. Try to see things the way other people do. When you can do this, you can solve problems better. You'll also feel less annoyed or frustrated.

What if you could read someone's mind? What if you were able to know their thoughts and feelings? This chapter will teach you the incredible Superpower of Empathy. To develop this superpower, you must learn how to be a detective.

How can you do this? In this chapter, you will see many activities. You can do them by yourself or with an adult. You will build empathy faster if you practice with an adult. Maybe they will finally understand why you do not want to clean your room!

Some of the activities also have fun power-up exercises. They will help you grow empathy faster.

What is Empathy

You can learn it to help you get along better with others and feel heard by others. Empathy means that you can understand and share other people's feelings.

How do you build empathy? You started building empathy the first moment you were cared for as a baby. The bonds you made in your first moments started you on this journey. It persisted as you developed, similar to how an individual looked after you while you were ill. Empathy is like a muscle that needs practice to grow. Remember when you were learning to read or write? You had to practice a lot, and you'll probably be practicing for many years. Building empathy is the same.

Empathy Check-In

We all have different ways of showing empathy. Understanding how you show empathy can help you find ways to grow. Empathy is like a muscle that takes time to get stronger. It is okay if you are not doing these things all the time. Our first activity will help you know what your empathy is like.

Consider how frequently you take each action after reading each statement. Be honest. There are no right or wrong answers. If you think you do it often, put an "x" on the line closer to "A lot." If you don't do it, put an "x" on the line closer to "Never."

1. I feel sad when my friend feels sad. Never _____ _____ A lot

2. When someone is upset, I think about how I would feel if it were me. Never _____ _____ A lot

3. I know what makes my friends happy. Never _____ _____ A lot

4. I get upset when someone is mean. Never _____ _____ A lot

5. I like to do nice things for others. Never _____ _____ A lot

6. I can understand someone else's opinion, even if I do not agree. Never _____ _____ A lot

7. I try to look at every side of something before deciding. Never _____ _____ A lot

8. I can cheer my friends when they win and I lose. Never _____ _____ A lot

9. I have a lot of pals that are not like me. Never _____ _____ A lot

10. I believe that both people can be right in an argument.

Never _____ _____ A lot

How did you do? The things you marked closer to "A lot" are ways you have more empathy. Pat yourself on the back. That is great!

Which one do you like to do the most?

_____ _____

_____ _____

_____

The things you marked closer to "Never" are ways you have less empathy. That's okay! We are going to work on building those.

Which one would you like to work on the most?

_____ _____

_____ _____

It's Not All About Us

Empathy is considering what other people could be experiencing. We can go through the same things but have different feelings about them. For example, if you miss the bus in the morning, you might be happy because you can ride in the car. Your dad might be frustrated because he will be late for work. Both of those feelings are okay.

To understand the other person's feelings, we need to put how we feel aside for a minute, which can be really hard! You have to be okay that the other person's feelings might be different. Remember, this is not forever. When we think about other people's feelings, they are more likely to think about ours in return.

Read each situation. Explain how you could put your feelings aside.

Example: Your grandmother gives you a gift you don't like.

I felt disappointed, but my grandmother felt excited to give me the gift.

I can put my feelings aside by remembering that getting a gift is special even if I don't like it.

1. You lose a game, but the other team wins. I feel _____, but the other team feels _____. I can put my feelings aside by _____.

2. Your room is messy, and your mom asks you to clean it. I feel _____, but my mom feels _____. I can put my feelings aside by _____.

3. Your dad makes something you don't like for dinner. I feel _____, but my dad feels _____. I can put my feelings aside by _____.

4. Your brother chooses a TV show that you don't like. I feel _____, but my brother feels _____. I can put my feelings aside by _____.

5. It's your turn to take the dog out, but you are very tired. I feel _____, but my dog feels _____. I can put my feelings aside by _____.

Caring Connects Us to Others

Consider your most recent illness. What made you feel better? It was probably something that another person did to help you. Did someone give you a glass of water or speak kind words? This act of caring is what pulls us together. When we do kind acts for people in our lives, it lets them know that we care and makes us feel good, too.

Thinking about others and caring about how they feel builds your empathy muscle. Whenever you do or say kind things, it builds your empathy and connects you to other people. This is good because we all need others in our lives. We would be pretty sad or lonely if we did not have our family or friends. So let's keep building our empathy muscles by looking at how we can care for others.

Caring Behaviors

When you show empathy, you feel what someone else feels. This can make you want to do something for them. If someone feels sad, you might want to hug them or get them a tissue. These helpful behaviors can make us feel good.

Read each situation. Highlight yes if the person is showing empathy and no if they aren't.

1. Putting an arm around a crying friend _____ yes _____ no

2. Watching a parent clean up _____ yes _____ no

3. Pushing a friend in a wheelchair _____ yes _____ no

4. Laughing at a hurt sister _____ yes _____ no

5. Helping a friend fix a toy _____ yes _____ no

6. Getting a Band-Aid for your brother _____ yes _____ no

7. Making fun of a friend's shirt _____ yes _____ no

Answer Solution: 1. Yes 2. No 3. Yes 4. No 5. Yes 6. Yes 7. No.

Think of a time you felt what a friend was feeling.

Write what you did and how you felt:

_____

_____

_____

_____

_____

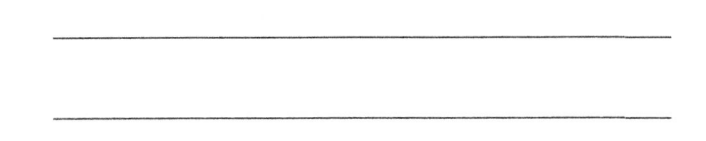

Our Caring Acts

There are many ways that you can show that you care. These are called caring acts. When you do caring acts, you let others know you are invested in the relationship. This is one of the best things about empathy. Sometimes, we get stuck doing the same kinds of caring acts. You can build your empathy muscle by trying different ways to show others you care.

Below are several caring acts. Think about how much you do each one. Draw hearts to indicate how often you do this. 4 hearts = a lot, 3 hearts = often, 2 hearts = sometimes, 1 heart = never.

SAY THANK YOU	
GIVE PEOPLE HUGS	
HELP PEOPLE	

INCLUDE PEOPLE WHO ARE LEFT OUT	
COMPLIMENT OTHERS	
CHEER PEOPLE UP	
GIVE GIFTS	
SHARE YOUR THINGS	
FIX BROKEN ITEMS	
WRITE THANK-YOU NOTES	

Look over the acts that you gave three or four hearts. Write why you like to do these things:

_____

_____

_____

Look over the acts you gave less than three hearts. Write why you don't do these things as much:

_____

_____

_____

Pick one act you don't do very much that you are willing to do more. Describe one thing you can do over the next week to perform this caring act:

_____

_____

_____

Do Something

After the week is over, write about the caring act you tried and how it made you feel:

_____

_____

_____

Empathy in Action

Showing care for others is one of the greatest parts of empathy, as it allows you to put your superpower to use. Imagine if Superman never used his ability to fly. That would be a shame, as this ability is something he can use anywhere to achieve great things. Empathy is the same. It's a superpower you have to use, not just talk about. In this section, we will practice using empathy in three areas: at home, at school, and in the world.

We will continue to level up our Empathy Superpower by focusing on the following:

Taking action: You will put empathy into action by thinking about what you can do for others. Empathy can be done everywhere!

Are you ready to show off your Empathy Superpower? Let's get going!

1. Empathy at Home

The first place you will practice your Empathy Superpower is at home. Some of you may have more than one! First, you'll practice empathy with the people you see daily. You might live with them. You can also do this with other close families you might not see every day but with whom you talk on the phone. You can also use empathy with people you only see sometimes, like your grandparents. These are all part of your family. Using empathy with our family makes everyone feel important. It also makes us feel closer to them. We tend to feel most connected to the people we live with.

Empathy makes your home calm. Who wants to argue all the time? We want to live where it is mostly calm. The skills in this section might help you get along better with your parents.

Animal Care

Animals need empathy, too! They cannot talk or tell us their feelings, but they still need us to be kind and care for them. Taking care of them is a great way to practice using empathy. Some people think showing empathy for animals is easier than for humans. It makes sense: animals are very loving and forgiving and don't argue with you.

Draw an animal that is part of your family. If you don't have a pet, that's okay. Think about some of the animals that live around you. Birds and frogs need kindness, too.

What did you draw?

_____

How could you show kindness to them?

_____

_____

_____

Are there other animals that could use your help? Maybe you can help animals at a local shelter or help a neighbor who can't walk their dog. Think about other things you could do to help animals that live around you.

_____

_____

Be Kind

The finest thing about empathy is how it helps us develop stronger bonds with the individuals we're passionate about. One way we can do this is to be kind. Kindness means showing someone you care about them. Anyone can be kind. It just takes a little time to think about the other person. A great thing about kindness is that when you show it, others will, too. This means that you'll get back each kind thing you do!

There are three ways you can be kind:

Actions: Things you do.

Sayings: Things you say.

Creations: Things you make.

Read over the list. Highlight the ones you like to do. If you can think of any others, write them in the blank spaces.

ACTIONS	SAYINGS	CREATIONS
Hold a door	Give a compliment	Bake cookies
Carry something	Write a friendly note	Make a card
Mow the lawn (if you're old enough!)	Say thank you	Write a song
Clean up trash	Tell a joke	Draw a picture
Read out loud	Say hello	Make a gift
Wash dishes	Say please	Cook someone's favorite food
Give a hug	Share a funny thing you heard someone say	Build something

List all the people you live with or who are in your family.

_____

_____

Pick two of those people. Think of two kind things you could do for each of them.

Person #1:

_____

1. _____

_____

2. _____

_____

Person #2:

_____

1. _____

_____

2. _____

_____

Do some of the kind things you listed. What did you do? How did it feel? How did the other person respond?

_____

_____

Helping Out

Adults do a lot of work at home. They cook. They clean. They do laundry. They take care of the children. That is their job, but as you get older, you should do some chores, too. You should also help your parents or family members if they are sick or hurt. Sharing chores helps bring you closer to your family. Helping also makes you feel good.

Read each situation. Think about what you could do to help out. Write your suggestions on the lines.

1. Your dad is sick with a cold.

   _____

   _____

2. Your grandparent can't read the small print.

   _____

   _____

3. Your uncle broke his arm and can't reach the TV remote.

   _____

   _____

4. Your little brother needs help with his homework.

   _____

   _____

5. Your mom is cooking dinner, but the dog needs to go out.

   _____

   _____

6. Your older cousin can't find the garbage bags.

   _____

   _____

7. Your grandparent needs help cleaning the sidewalk.

_____

_____

2. Empathy at School

School is another place where you spend a lot of time. You can practice using your Empathy superpower there, too. This means knowing how other children your age might feel or see things. School can be the first place we meet people who are not like us. We can have different skin colors. We can have different types of families or holidays. We can even have different likes and dislikes.

Empathy for people at school helps us get along with them. Empathy also makes us feel safe. Imagine if your ideas differed from everyone else's, and no one listened to them. This would probably make you feel angry or unheard. This section will focus on showing people at school we care.

School Snags

School can be frustrating sometimes. Sometimes events don't happen the way that we anticipate. Our classmates also have things go wrong. Empathy at school means we can also think about how they feel. We can also think about what we can do to show we care.

Read each situation. Write what you can do to show empathy.

1. Conner does not score during the soccer game at recess.

    How do you think Conner feels?

    _____

    How can you show you care?

    _____

    _____

2. Stacy doesn't do well on the math test.

    How do you think Stacy feels?

    _____

    How can you show you care?

    _____

    _____

3. Kieran tells the class their dog died.

How do you think Kieran feels?

_____

How can you show you care?

_____

_____

4. Hamza is playing alone during recess.

   How do you think Hamza feels?

   _____

   How can you show you care?

   _____

   _____

5. Mia tells you they are moving far away.

   How do you think Mia feels?

   _____

   How can you show you care?

   _____

   _____

6. Caesar trips and falls in front of the class.

   How do you think Caesar feels?

   _____

   How can you show you care?

   _____

   _____

7. Hanya throws up in class.

   How do you think Hanya feels?

   _____

   How can you show you care?

   _____

   _____

Over the next few days, show empathy to a classmate you don't know very well. Maybe you can act kindly or get to know them better. Tell me about it.

_____

_____

3. Empathy in the World

We have done many activities practicing empathy at home and school. These are places where you spend most of your time. As you get older, you will expand where you go.

You will learn that you are a small part of a much bigger world. You'll learn about others who do not live near you. They might speak other languages or have other skills. They might eat other types of foods. Regardless of where they are from or how they appear, we should work on being friendly to everyone.

This type of empathy is the hardest kind. It might be challenging to understand other people's perspectives when they are different from ours. We can't always tell how they feel or see things. For example, some children don't have a school to go to. We might think that is great, but they might feel like they are missing out. In this section, we will practice showing empathy to those in our community and the world.

Community Helpers

Our community is made up of many different people. We don't always notice them, but what they do makes other people's lives easier. Have you ever thought about who picks up the garbage? Who changes a streetlight? Who makes sure the park is safe? All these things are done by community helpers or people who care for others.

Read each job description. Draw a line to the person you believe could do the job.

1. I bring mail or packages.

2. I grow food.

3. I help people borrow books.

4. I cut people's hair.

5. I protect things from fire.

6. I clean and fix teeth.

7. I help animals when they are sick.

a. Hairstylist/Barber

b. Veterinarian

c. Postal worker

d. Dentist

e. Farmer

f. Librarian

g. Firefighter

Answer Solution One. c Two. e Three. f Four. a Five. g Six. d Seven. b

Look over the list. Can you think of other community helpers, not on the list?

_____

_____

What might occur if we lacked these helpers?

_____

_____

How would things be different?

_____

_____

Write a thank-you letter to someone who helps in

your community. What could you say to them?

_____

_____

Caring about things in your community is part of empathy. It means telling others about problems that are going on. Even children like you can get involved! Imagine that a local skate park does not have lights. As a result of this, children would get hurt after dark. You could ask your parents to help you write a letter to the town hall asking them to add lights.

Think about the issue you picked in the last activity. One way to bring attention to an issue is to write a letter. Using the guide below, write a letter to a person or group about your issue. Ask an adult to assist you in writing your letter. You may either note it down or email it.

1. Who are you writing to? It is okay if you don't know their name. You can use their title, like "principal," "president," or "senator."

_____

_____

2. Describe the issue.

_____

_____

3. Write two or three things you learned about it.

_____

_____

4. Give some solutions to the problem.

_____

_____

5. What do you hope will be changed?

_____

_____

6. What would you like them to do?

_____

_____

7. Sign your letter.

_____

_____

Are there any other ways you can help your community? What would you want to do?

_____

_____

Getting along with (or caring for) others is important when building relationships. Teaching your child creative ways to build their social skills can help. In the next chapter, your child will learn to be themselves.

Chapter Nine:

I'll Be Myself and Nothing Else

A tired bird came to sit on a branch. The bird rested, taking in the view from its perch and the protection it provided from predators. A strong wind started blowing just as the bird was getting used to the support and safety it provided, and the tree swayed so violently that it appeared the branch would snap in half.

But the bird was not worried because it was aware of two crucial facts. The first is that even without the branch, the bird could fly and stay safe thanks to the power of its own two wings. The second was that it knew numerous other branches on which it could temporarily rest.

This little narrative teaches us a lot about ourselves

and our bravery and self-assurance. We are much more powerful than most of us think in daily life, and when we can simply let go of the physical structures that keep us grounded, we begin to understand how far we can fly under our power.

There are numerous so-called limbs and oaks that we depend on. And while we do require recovery and shelter from time to time, as we mature, we might also discover that these security sources aren't always reliable—what is truly lasting and permanent is within us, in the form of positive self-esteem and belief in our own unique abilities (Grubb, 2019).

Confidence means having faith in oneself and one's abilities—not arrogantly, but realistically and securely. Being confident does not imply feeling superior to others. It's a quiet inner knowing that you can do it.

Practice Positive Self-Talk

Make your child believe they can overcome challenges instead of telling them to hide their negative feelings. Put differently, toxic optimism, which involves continual suppression of unpleasant feelings, is harmful over time.

Self-talk is talking to oneself; it's something most people do, whether they're aware of it or not. By encouraging your child to use it, you can help them feel more confident and self-assured. Your child will be happier, more self-assured, and in better physical and mental condition if they practice positive self-talk (Lakhotia, 2023).

If you have children, encourage them to approach every situation with optimism because it lifts their spirits. Engaging in positive self-talk can broaden their perspectives, aid them in achieving challenging goals, and also makes them feel happier. Negative thoughts or beliefs can sabotage your child's confidence.

Self-doubt is common among many preteens and teenagers. Numerous unfavorable thoughts could weigh a child down and weaken their self-esteem. Self-talk has more impact on our mental health than we know — for example, children using positive self-talk can develop confidence and acquire the relevant skills to deal with trying circumstances. Acquiring positive self-talk skills helps children start a conversation or seek support when facing obstacles.

Here are practical examples of self-talk situations:

If you're angry because of a particular problem, consider saying, "This is a task I can complete" or "Difficult times are temporary, so there's no point worrying."

If things don't turn out as planned, say, "I can turn the situation around," "I can learn to do it better," or "I can ask my caregivers for support."

These are ways children can practice positive self-talk.

Use **I AM**. This positive self-talk activity encourages using I AM with the most appropriate adjective. Examples include, "I am wise and fearless," "I am a wonderful child capable of handling difficult tasks," or "I am content and perfect."

If your child tries this self-talk activity, they'll start seeing results after a month of practice. The I AM activity boosts confidence, making it one of the best exercises for encouraging self-talk in children (Lakhotia, 2023).

Write and Read Positive Self-Talk Statements. Keep a notebook close by so you may record the encouraging things you tell yourself. Every morning, take a seat and read it out loud.

Hang Positive Affirmation Papers on the Bedroom Wall. Ask your parents to purchase some vibrant sketch pens and new notebooks next time they go shopping. Write some of the most effective affirmations for positive self-talk in a variety of colors on each sheet of paper.

I AM BECOMING MORE CONFIDENT EVERYDAY

Stick all your completed papers on the wall of your bedroom. They'll be ready for you when you get impatient with something and need a break.

Mirror Positive Self-Talk Activities. Try one experiment at home tomorrow morning: reaffirm the good things you are saying to yourself while looking yourself up in the mirror.

Keep your eyes on yourself. You'll feel good saying the passionate, encouraging affirmation. You'll experience confidence and strength.

Don't worry if your child is doubting; you can increase their positive self-talk by encouraging them to think positively.

Create Awareness. Making your child conscious is the first step in helping them start using positive self-talk. The impact of self-talk on our everyday life is something that most of us are ignorant of, even as adults. So, it might look like a very foreign idea to your child.

Describe self-talk and tell your child how it affects them. Then, ask them to identify their perceived areas of strength and weakness. Ask them how they deal with their emotions concerning a particular task. Is there a method they can use to make it simpler or more effective? These queries help people become conscious of their emotional states.

Consider telling your child to record their feelings in a chart or journal to recognize what requires changes.

Survey Feelings. Encourage your child to record at least five of their inner thoughts each day. Help them analyze their feelings. Start working actively on it once your child learns self-talk. Allow them to carry paper and a pen at all times.

Analyzing thoughts helps simplify finding repeated habits. Children often experience the same thoughts repeatedly, even when having varied thoughts throughout the day. For example, they may feel unhappy before going to school or thrilled after engaging in physical activity. Try to spot these behavioral patterns in your child.

Spot Hostile Self-Talk. Your child should be adept at identifying harmful self-talk; this is crucial because it helps them think favorably. It could be challenging because it calls for intense concentration and the ability to recognize bad thoughts that masquerade as positive ones (Lakhotia, 2023).

Negative words do not necessarily accompany negative thoughts. For example, "I can't do this homework" is an unfavorable statement. Other negative assertions include: "That boy is smarter than me" or "I won't pass the exam even if I studied all night."

Learn to admit negative self-talk if you hope to overcome it.

Change Negative Statements to Positive Affirmations. Advise your children to turn bad feelings into positive ones. They can do it through internal dialogue or self-talk, although it takes practice to master the method.

Ask your older children to treat themselves with the same kindness they show others.

Use Favorable Affirmations. Inspire your child to use encouraging words to improve their lives. For example, if your child feels they can't resolve a puzzle or answer math issues, tell them to use a positive statement like I may not understand this, but I can answer it with my parent's or teacher's help.

Positive comments support your child's self-confidence, so get into a habit of using them.

Include Self-Talk in Daily Conversation. Your child will better understand what self-talk is and how it impacts them by having regular conversations about good thinking.

Asking how your child feels and encouraging them to be positive may help change their negative thoughts into positive ones. You can also talk about your bad ideas and how you deal with them.

Your child will feel at ease in your presence and be willing to express their feelings if you have an open chat.

Morning Meditations

Good morning, dear, and welcome to a brand new day! Did you know that how you feel right after you wake up is often how you'll feel for the rest of the day?

We'll prepare to welcome the energy of the day by bringing some words into our hearts to help us feel good whenever we need them.

Make sure you're completely comfortable wherever you are, and then close your eyes if you want.

Let's take deep breaths together: a big, slow inhale, followed by a soft, gentle exhale. One more: a deep, slow inhale, followed by a soft, gentle exhale. Great!

Let's put both hands on your heart in whatever way feels comfortable, and let's say these words together, out loud or in your head, whichever you prefer:

"I am adored. I am safe. I'm in a good mood. I am gentle. I'm cool. I am useful. I can do difficult things."

Repeat them as often as you wish.

Feel the warmth of your hands on your heart and smile to yourself. Then, if it feels right, give yourself a big hug and tell yourself, out loud or in your head, "Today will be a good day because I am here on earth, and I am loved."

Take a deep breath in, then exhale. Perhaps, stretch and yawn. Have a fantastic day!

Evening Meditations

Is it hard to turn off your mind when it's time for bed? Do you feel wired instead of tired? Some days are fast and busy. Others are slower and more relaxed. When it's time to go to sleep, taking a peaceful pause is the perfect way to feel calm and relaxed. Just remember, you can feel peaceful whenever you choose.

Children have a special chance to meditate right before bed; this is the time to stop playing games, forget the day's activities, relax, and sleep. Meditation is skipping tasks and entering a state of calm (Kim, 2019). Encourage your children to include a three or five-minute meditation in their pre-sleep routines.

In contrast to other meditation techniques, children enjoy a technique called loving-kindness because it is illustrative, keeps them focused, and makes them feel good. Through the use of loving-kindness meditation, children can express their emotions and sense other people's feelings of compassion, kindness, and love by focusing on them or sending them nice thoughts.

Loving-kindness is a sort of emotional and spiritual practice in which we offer ourselves and others love, respect, and care through channeling pleasant feelings, sincerity, and good wishes.

Individuals who consistently engage in loving-kindness yoga feel happier concerning themselves and everyone else. It stimulates the brain in the same way that charitable deeds do, producing happy sentiments that progress to beneficial conduct.

Keep loving-kindness group sessions with children brief and simple. Consider using these phrases to practice this activity in its most straightforward form (Kim, 2019).

"May you be well."

"May you be secure and guarded."

"May you have joy and peace."

The three phrases refer to the following human groupings:

Oneself.

Someone the child shares a deep bond with—a relative, teacher, caretaker, or friend.

A creature or element of the environment—a cat, a river, or a mountain.

All beings.

Feel free to modify the phrases. Depending on a child's developmental capabilities, their caregivers may change the phrases and broaden the categories.

Bedtime Meditation Script

Pick a place without outside interruptions when mediating since it's a silent activity. The floor, your bed, a pillow, a chair, or a mat are suitable places to sit or lie down to meditate (Kim, 2019).

You may prevent visual distractions by closing your eyes or focusing your attention a few feet forward and downward.

Breathe deeply into your belly for a long, complete moment.

Say aaah as you take a deep breath out.

Inhale deeply once more, followed by another satisfying sigh of relaxation.

As you're doing this, you're unwinding and letting your body sink into the bed and becoming relaxed.

If you'd like, you can put one or both of your hands over your heart.

Picture a warm, glistening light—like sunlight—bringing love and kindness to your heart.

Let's start by being friendly to ourselves and keeping in mind our built-in goodness and kindness.

Consider confessing these phrases. "I am healthy." "May I be content and joyful." "May I be safe and protected."

Repeat each line slowly—give yourself at least five seconds between each statement to sense the connection.

Consider making Grandma the recipient of your kindness. Imagine Grandma sitting on her favorite chair by the window.

"May Grandma be healthy."

"May she be happy and protected."

"May she be content and at peace."

Extend your loving kindness to the rainforests, where trees produce the clean air we breathe and shaded habitats for different tribes and animals.

"May the rainforests prosper." "May they be safe."

"May there be joy and peace in every rainforest." "May all creatures live long and flourish."

"May all beings experience happiness and stability." Repeat these words a few times silently.

Helpful Exercises for Staying Calm and in Charge of My Feelings

Relaxation Techniques for Child

Locate a quiet area free of distractions. You don't have to complete all of them. Keep track of how long you're engaged, and try again later.

Candle and Flower. This straightforward relaxation technique promotes deep breathing.

Assume you have a fragrant flower in one hand and a slow-burning candle in the other.

Slowly inhale through your nose while smelling the flower.

As you blow out the candle, exhale slowly through your mouth.

Repeat a few times.

Lemon. This relaxation exercise helps relieve muscle tension.

Pretend you're holding a lemon.

Pick a lemon with each hand and reach up to the tree.

Squeeze the lemons vigorously to extract all of the juice — squeeze, squeeze, squeeze!

Throw the lemons to the ground and take a deep breath.

Then, repeat until you have enough lemonade for a glass.

Shake your hands out to relax after your final squeeze and throw!

Lazy Cat. This exercise helps to relieve muscle tension.

Assume you are a sluggish cat who has just awoken

from a long nap.

Have a good yawn and a meow.

Now, relax like a cat stretching your arms, legs, and back.

Feather/Statue. This exercise helps to relieve muscle tension.

For about ten seconds, imagine that you are a feather floating through the air.

You suddenly freeze and turn into a statue. Keep still!

Then, as you slowly relax, transform back into the floating feather.

Repeat, finishing as a floaty feather in a relaxed state.

Stress Ball. This exercise relaxes your muscles and massages your hands.

Fill balloons with dry lentils or rice to make your own stress ball(s).

Squeeze and release the ball(s) in one or both hands.

Play around with squeezing the ball.

Find a method that works for you by adjusting your

squeezes' speed, pressure, and timing.

Turtle. This exercise helps to relieve muscle tension.

Assume you're a turtle taking a slow, relaxed turtle walk.

Oh no, it's begun to rain! For about ten seconds, curl up tight under your shell.

The sun has returned, so come out of your shell and resume your relaxing walk.

Repeat several times, finishing with a walk to relax your body.

Creative Calm-Down Tips for Children

The difficulties of growing up can be unpleasant, and your child may not always respond well to deep breathing, but these calm-down ideas may help your child unwind or reduce stress.

Picture a calm place. Visualization helps lessen stress, and it is helpful for a variety of demographics. Ask your kid to dim their vision so they can picture a peaceful scene.

Once they have a general idea of what it feels like to be there, guide them as they develop a mental image of it.

Drink enough water. Dehydration is a major cause of the decline in mental performance among children (GoZen, 2017).

Give your child a glass of cool water, and encourage them to take gentle sips. Experiment with them and see how their mental health improves.

Try downward-facing dog yoga. This pose helps engage the muscles in the arms, legs, and core and strengthens the nervous system.

As a result of the body's fight-or-flight response, this stretch enables muscles to start burning surplus blood glucose.

Jump rope. Set a 2-minute timer, mix some audio, and tell your kid to dance along with it. Hope scotch is an exceptional substitute if your child can't jump rope.

Jog. If you want to reduce stress, running or jogging occasionally may help. While kids respond differently to exercise, your child may feel better and handle tension after a brisk workout.

Count to five. While dealing with difficulties or problems, instruct your child to relax their gaze and count from one to five when facing challenges or handling difficult situations.

This five-second meditation may help reset a child's brain and form a fresh perspective when facing a potentially harmful circumstance.

Jump high. Challenge your children to a competition to see who can leap higher, faster, or slower. Engaging in physical activity is an excellent way to help your child release stress.

Sing out loud. Everyone knows the wonderful comfort they get listening to their favorite music. Singing aloud helps release endorphins, the feel-good brain chemical, even when we sing off-pitch (GoZen, 2017).

Blow bubbles. Blowing bubbles might help your child regulate their respiration and mood. Popping bubbles while running around is as entertaining as blowing them.

Have a warm bath. Nothing is more soothing after a hard day at work than relaxing in a warm bathtub with the lamps dimmed and no interruptions.

Children experience the same thing — take advantage of the opportunity to assist your child in relaxing during bath time after a long day of activities.

Introduce bath toys and give your child as much time as necessary to relax.

Opt for a chill shower. Like warm baths, cold showers are beneficial to the body's ability to heal. Aside from reducing muscle inflammation, taking a cold bath helps improve mood.

A study on winter swimmers found that regular dips into cold water could reduce stress, fatigue, sadness, and poor moods (GoZen, 2017).

Make a bracelet. Crafting can assist children in achieving a sense of flow in an activity. Encourage your child to use the same reasoning for crocheting, knitting, or any hobby that enables them to enjoy life.

Ride a bike. Children's bicycles seem to have lost their usefulness. Since paved trails and bike lanes have been installed in metropolitan areas, bike riding has become more secure than before and may be a powerful way to relieve stress.

The whole family may participate in it, and it is easy on the joints while encouraging balance and fitness.

Get a coloring break. Children get access to coloring pages for a reason—It gives them focus and may be a great mindfulness exercise that reduces anxiety.

Bring your child along when shopping so they can pick out their crayons, markers, and coloring books.

Embrace painting. Painting diverts the brain's attention from stressors. Participating in artwork has been associated with improved stress tolerance in general (GoZen, 2017).

Have your child experiment with grooming gel artwork on a vinyl shower curt in the garden if being outside bothers them out.

Snuff a candle. Your kid flicks out a flame while you lit one.

Relight the fire and place it farther from your child so they must breathe in deeply before exhaling.

Turn it into a game—this helps your child practice deep breathing.

Watch fish. Have you ever questioned why many

medical facilities—including hospitals—have fish tanks?

According to studies, observing fish flow in a pool lowers blood pressure and pulse rate (GoZen, 2017). The impact is greater the bigger the fish tank is.

Take your child to a nearby lake, fish hatchery, or aquarium the next time they need some help unwinding.

Do a backward counting from 100. Your child can divert their attention from whatever is annoying them by counting.

The added mental difficulty of counting backward keeps their brain from being overworked.

Recite a mantra. Along with your child, come up with a calming phrase that you can both repeat.

Saying I am comfortable or calm may be effective, but you will do better with creativity.

Make the mantra special for you and your child.

Have deep belly breathing. Feeling stressed makes people breathe poorly. Help your child picture their stomach as a balloon.

Encourage them to inhale deeply to inflate the

balloon and exhale to deflate it. Watch the results after five repetitions of this straightforward procedure.

Walk through the park. Scientists have shown that taking a walk in nature might boost thinking skills and lower stress levels.

If you don't have fifty minutes to spare as the researchers did, your child might benefit from a fifteen-minute nature walk (GoZen, 2017).

Visit your relaxing area. When children feel out of control, having a calm-down space in the house can help.

Making the place comfortable encourages your child to use it. Stir the glitter jar. Your child's brain and body can reset themselves if you give them something to focus on.

Talk it over. Children who can express their feelings can tell you what's troubling them. Rather than attempting to resolve the issue on their own, your child learns to depend on you for support or counsel.

Design a wall decor. Using cut-out pictures from magazines, newspapers, or internet design templates, your child can produce beautiful wall ornaments. What counts in this activity is the creation process, not the product.

Make a vision board. Cut out magazine articles and pictures relevant to your child's goals and interests. After that, instruct them to attach these words and images to a poster board in their room—this creative process helps children reflect on their dreams (or what they want to achieve).

Hug your kid. Hugging increases the body's natural synthesis of oxytocin, the hormone enhancing the performance of the immune system.

Recent studies have found that a 20-second embrace can decrease blood pressure, boost emotional well-being, and reduce stress (GoZen, 2017).

Fold tissue paper. Being one of their favorite activities, many babies know crinkle paper. Apart from producing a pleasing sound, the texture variations in your child's palm cause the brain to receive sensory information in a different way than it would under stressful conditions.

Picture your best self. Inspire your kid to desire a great feat using this activity. Encourage them to write their aspirations for the coming week, month, or year and devise ways of achieving them.

Inflate a pinwheel. Prioritize controlled exhalation

above deep inhaling when breathing on a pinwheel. Tell your child to turn the pinwheel slowly, swiftly, and slowly to alter the speed at which air leaves their lungs.

Use putty. Electric signals in the nervous system shift away from the anxiety areas when a kid plays on silicone. Use homemade putty or buy some from the shop.

Try pottery. Like sculpting with clay or tossing pots, putty sends electrical impulses to a child's brain. Also, it encourages effective teaching, a desirable circumstance that enables your kid to learn by doing.

Publish it. It can significantly improve older children's mood when they are able to write about their feelings without being concerned that they would be read aloud.

Allow your child to keep a journal where they can record their feelings and preserve them in a safe place. Inform them that unless they directly request it, you won't read it.

Practice Gratitude. Writing gratitude journals may enhance academic achievement and lessen stress outside of the classroom. To help your child differentiate their journaling activities, keep a different notebook for things for which they are grateful.

Describe feelings. Children may not notice their negative emotions when overwhelmed. If your child is easily disturbed or worried, encourage them to name the feeling and talk back about it. For example, instead of combating their perfectionism, you can work with your child to confront the issue.

Swing on a back-and-forth rocking chair. The rhythmic motion of rocking relieves stress and strengthens the knees and core.

Swinging your children in a rocking chair or allowing them to do it themselves will help calm their feelings.

Squat. This activity helps the body eliminate stress hormones. Encourage your children to squat for ten seconds and repeat the exercise three times daily. The muscles contract during and relax, making the body release feel-good hormones.

Squish bubble wrap. Anybody who has ever received a box in the mail will confirm that rows upon rows of bubble wrap may be joyfully burst. Many merchants and dollar stores sell the same material, which you can cut into manageable pieces for stress relief.

Enjoy some music. Music has a profound influence on one's emotions, sleep, stress, and fear. Set the mood in your house, automobile, or child's room with a range of musical genres.

Schedule a dancing party. Your children will have more fun being active if you combine some physical activity. If your child is having an awful day, pop on some tunes and have a fun time in the living room to see how their mood changes.

Make a configuration change. How often have you encouraged yourself to change when feeling depressed or having strong emotions?

Your child might need a new environment to relax; if you're inside, go outside. If you're tired of your everyday spaces, go to a new place to walk around. Changing the environment may help improve your child's mood.

Take a walk. Walking helps some people unwind; it provides fresh air and relaxes the body. Take your child for a walk to test if they will discuss their feelings with you.

Plan an enjoyable activity. If you're worried, it could feel like the world is ending, and the walls are closing in around you. Some children need to focus on re-establishing their internal dialogue—let your child participate when planning a pleasant family activity.

Any subject that encourages children to consider the future or provides them with something to anticipate can be helpful.

Mix the dough. Worldwide, grandmothers will attest to the stress-relieving benefits of baking bread. Your child can get their hands messy by rotating and pressing dough using straightforward online recipes.

The interesting part of this exercise is you'll get handmade bread!

Share the knowledge you gain from this book with your friends. You acquire knowledge by educating others; tell your pals about what you have learned about controlling your feelings, anger, and anxiety. Your buddies will be better at controlling their emotions and sympathizing with others.

Final Words

It takes time to develop the ability to manage our thoughts, feelings, and behaviors. We are subjected to events that evaluate and enhance our capacity to regulate our moods and sentiments in tricky times from a tender age.

Children's development of self-regulation may include learning proper ways to deal with setbacks instead of tantrums or expressing their anxiety without breaking down by asking for assistance.

These instances highlight the significance of self-control skills. Self-regulation is someone's ability to manage their emotions and mental processes to foster goal-oriented activities.

If a child's social talents function correctly, they may recognize the nature or origin of their impulse, reduce its intensity, and possibly understand methods for preventing reacting to it. Self-regulation talents, in a larger sense, enable kids to practice self-control.

Understanding how kids learn these abilities can help parents teach and reinforce them at home. According to studies, executive functions and interpersonal and emotional managerial skills, including self-regulation, significantly influence school preparation and early student achievement.

Also, since their minds and bodies can control and react less irregularly, children will be more bonded, more adept at solving issues, and healthier.

Creating a comfortable and encouraging setting for your kid to develop and apply self-regulation strategies is crucial for long-term success, mainly if your child exhibits auditory overflow or executive function issues.

One of your roles as a parent is to encourage your kid to learn self-control and provide feedback so that they may discover new ways to control or improve their moods.

This book contains practical and entertaining worksheets, activities, and games designed to teach kids self-regulation.

I hope that this book has assisted you in overcoming self-regulation challenges and developing a more positive personality. Now that you are equipped with all the tools, put them to use. Please write a review on Amazon if you found this book helpful.

References

APA. (n.d.). *Anger.* https://www.apa.org/topics/anger#:~:text=Anger%20is%20an%20emotion%20characterized,excessive%20anger%20can%20cause%20problems.

Biswas, S.K. (2020, September 3). Why Do We Shout in Anger? ILLUMINATION. https://medium.com/illumination/why-do-we-shout-in-anger-84859c04da04

Childhood 101. (n.d.). *Exploring Emotions Jenga Game.* https://childhood101.com/exploring-emotions-jenga-game/

Cikanavicius, D. (2018, August 13). *Childhood Trauma: How We Learn to Lie, Hide, and Be Inauthentic.* https://psychcentral.com/blog/psychology-self/2018/08/trauma-hiding#1

Clear View. (n.d.). *STOPP Technique.* https://www.anjclearview.co.uk/stop

Contentment Questing. (n.d.). *Benefits of Nature Walks.* https://contentmentquesting.com/benefits-of-nature-walks/

Day, N. (2022, February 28). List of Emotions & Feelings for Children | + Free PDF Emotions List. Raising an Extraordinary Person. https://hes-extraordinary.com/list-of-emotions-and-feelings-for-children

Dolgoff, S. (2020, April 29). Experts Agree That Baking Is One of the Best Things You Can Do to Relieve Stress Right Now. Good Housekeeping. https://www.goodhousekeeping.com/health/wellness/g32226840/stress-relief-activities/

Felman, A. (2020, January 11). *What to know about anxiety.* https://www.medicalnewstoday.com/articles/323454

Goldstein, C. (2016, February 2). What to Do (and Not Do) When Children Are Anxious. Child Mind Institute. https://childmind.org/article/what-to-do-and-not-do-when-children-are-anxious/

GoZen. (2017, April 19). *50 activities to calm your angry child.* https://www.mother.ly/parenting/50-calm-down-ideas-to-try-with-children-of-all-ages/

Grubb, J. (2019, September 9). Teaching Our Children To Be

Proud of Themselves: More Encouragement, Less Praise. Collin County Moms. https://collincounty.momcollective.com/parenting/teaching-our-children-to-be-proud-of-themselves-more-encouragement-less-praise

Help Guide. (n.d.). *Effective Communication.* https://www.helpguide.org/articles/relationships-communication/effective-communication.htm

Holland, K. (2022, June 28). *Everything You Need to Know About Anxiety.* https://www.healthline.com/health/anxiety

Hudson Therapy. (2019, May 24). *How to make your own mindfulness jar.* https://www.google.com/amp/s/hudsontherapygroup.com/blog/how-to-make-your-own-mindfulness-jar%3fformat=amp

Johns Hopkins. (n.d.). *9 Benefits of Yoga.* https://www.hopkinsmedicine.org/health/wellness-and-prevention/9-benefits-of-yoga

Children's Health. (2018, August 5). *Taking charge of anger.* https://www.childrenhealth.org/ETCH/en/children/anger.html?WT.ac=k-ra

Kim, S. (2019, June 18). *Goodnight Metta: A Bedtime Meditation for Children.* https://tricycle.org/article/bedtime-meditation-for-children/

Lakhotia, P. (2023, February 7). *Positive Self-Talk For Children: Its Importance And Ways To Teach.* https://www.momjunction.com/articles/positive-self-talk-for-children-examples-importance_00708881/

Meraki Lane. (n.d.). *Helping Children Cope: 14 Cognitive Behavioral Therapy Activities for Children.* https://www.merakilane.com/helping-children-cope-14-cognitive-behavioral-therapy-activities-for-children/

MHC. (2014, September 12). *What is Body Mapping?* http://www.musicianshealthcollective.com/blog/2014/9/11/what-is-body-mapping

Miller, K. (2019, May 21). *39 Communication Games and Activities for Children and Students.* https://positivepsychology.com/communication-activities-adults-students/

Morin, A. (2021, October 17). *7 Ways to Help a Child Cope With Anger.* https://www.verywellfamily.com/ways-to-help-an-angry-child-1094976

NHS. (n.d.). *Helping your child with anger issues.* https://www.nhs.uk/mental-health/children-and-young-adults/advice-for-parents/help-your-child-with-anger-issues/

Raypole, C. (2022, December 5). *How to Do a Body Scan Meditation (and Why You Should).* https://www.healthline.com/health/body-scan-meditation

Rouse, M. (n.d.). *How Can We Help Children With Self-Regulation?* https://childmind.org/article/can-help-children-self-regulation/

SDK First. (n.d.). *Anger-Management/Emotional Regulation.* https://sdchildrenfirst.com/expertcorner/knowledgecenter/anger/

World Health Organization. (2021, October 12). *Stress.* https://www.who.int/news-room/questions-and-answers/item/stress#:~:text=Stress%20can%20be%20defined%20as,to%20your%20overall%20well%2Dbeing.

Wow Parenting. (n.d.). *Activities for children to release their stress.* https://wowparenting.com/blog/activity-for-kids-to-bust-stress/

You are mom. (2019, February 17). *My Child Is Always Yelling: What Can I Do?* https://youaremom.com/children/child-is-always-yelling/

Printed in Great Britain
by Amazon